QuickCook

QuickCook
One Pot

Recipes by Emma Lewis

Every dish, three ways—you choose!
30 minutes | 20 minutes | 10 minutes

An Hachette UK Company
www.hachette.co.uk

First published in Great Britain in 2012 by Hamlyn,
a division of Octopus Publishing Group Ltd
Endeavour House, 189 Shaftesbury Avenue
London WC2H 8JY
www.octopusbooks.co.uk
www.octopusbooksusa.com

Distributed in the US by Hachette Book Group USA
237 Park Avenue, New York NY 10017 USA

Distributed in Canada by Canadian Manda Group
165 Dufferin Street, Toronto, Ontario, Canada M6K 3H6

ISBN 978-0-600-62508-7

Printed and bound in China

10 9 8 7 6 5 4 3 2 1

Standard level spoon and cup measurements are used in all recipes.

Ovens should be preheated to the specified temperature. If using a convection oven,
follow the manufacturer's instructions for adjusting the time and temperature.
Broilers should also be preheated.

This book includes dishes made with nuts and nut derivatives. It is advisable for
those with known allergic reactions to nuts and nut derivatives and those who may
be potentially vulnerable to these allergies, such as pregnant and nursing mothers,
people with weakened immune systems, the elderly, babies, and children, to avoid
dishes made with nuts and nut oils.

It is also prudent to check the labels of prepared ingredients for the possible inclusion
of nut derivatives.

The United States Department of Agriculture (USDA) advises that eggs should not
be consumed raw. This book contains some dishes made with raw or lightly cooked
eggs. It is prudent for more vulnerable people, such as pregnant and nursing mothers,
people with weakened immune systems, the elderly, babies, and young children, to
avoid uncooked or lightly cooked dishes made with eggs.

Contents

Introduction

30 20 10—Quick, Quicker, Quickest

This book offers a new and flexible approach to planning meals for busy cooks, letting you choose the recipe option that best fits the time you have available. Inside, you will find 360 dishes that will inspire and motivate you to get cooking every day of the year. All the recipes take a maximum of 30 minutes to cook. Some take as little as 20 minutes and, amazingly, many take only 10 minutes. With a little preparation, you can easily try out one new recipe from this book each night and slowly you will be able to build a wide and exciting portfolio of recipes to suit your needs.

How Does it Work?

Every recipe in the QuickCook series can be cooked one of three ways: a 30-minute version, a 20-minute version, or a superquick-and-easy 10-minute version. At the beginning of each chapter, you'll find recipes listed by time. Choose a dish based on how much time you have and turn to that page.

You'll find the main recipe in the middle of the page accompanied by a beautiful photograph, as well as two time-variation recipes below.

If you enjoy your chosen dish, why not go back and cook the other time-variation options at a later date? So, if you liked the 20-minute Crunchy Berry Brûlée, but only have 10 minutes to spare this time around, you'll find a way to cook it using quick ingredients or clever shortcuts.

If you love the ingredients and flavors of the 10-minute Chile Shrimp Noodles, why not try something more substantial, such as the 20-minute Chile Shrimp and Lime Couscous, or be inspired to make a more elaborate version, such as the Chile Shrimp Bisque? Alternatively, browse through all 360 delicious recipes, find something that catches your eye, then cook the version that fits your time frame.

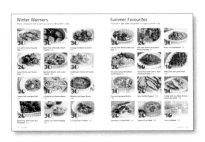

Or, for easy inspiration, turn to the gallery on pages 12–19 to get an instant overview by themes, such as Winter Warmers or Summer Favorites.

QuickCook online

To make life even easier, you can use the special code on each recipe page to e-mail yourself a recipe card for printing, or e-mail a text-only shopping list to your phone.

ONE-POUL-JEI

QuickCook One Pot

With so many of us living busy lives these days, cooking dinner is enough of an effort without having to tackle a mountain of dishes afterward. One-pot dishes are simple to prepare— from an easy salad tossed together in a bowl, to quickly cooking some meat and vegetables and then simmering in a flavorful liquid. Once dinner is finished cleaning up is easy. All the recipes in this book require just one cooking utensil, and because everything is ready in just 30 minutes or less, you can spend more time relaxing and less time working in the kitchen.

Choosing the Right Pot, Pan, or Dish

Casserole Dish: A heavy-based casserole dish is perfect for many one-pot dishes and there are plenty that are attractive enough to bring from the stove to the table for a dinner party. They are best for making making moist dishes, such as stews or curries. Start off by sautéing meat, onions, or other vegetables to get a rich base flavor, then add flavorings, maybe tomatoes, stock, or a splash of cream, cover, and leave the dish to cook by itself. You can also find shallow dishes that are great for cooking rice-base dishes. The best pots are Dutch ovens made from cast iron, which is great at retaining heat and ensuring even cooking. They can be pricy to buy, but they are an investment that should last you a lifetime.

Saucepan: Every cook should have a large saucepan in their kitchen. Ideally, get a heavy pan so you can double up and use it for sautéing, too. A large pan will give you the space you need to cook soup or pasta for the whole family, or any other recipe that requires a lot of liquid.

Skillet: To give food a really robust, caramelized flavor you would find in a restaurant, you need a good skillet or sauté pan. To make sure that food doesn't burn when cooking, look for pans with a heavy bottom. Sticking is often a problem when sautéing, so try using a cast-iron pan and heating it until it is smoking hot—the heat will help prevent food from sticking—or you can use a nonstick pan. Sauté pans are deeper than skillets, lettin you cook more gently and making it easier to add a little stock or other liquid. You can also buy sauté pans with a lid, which lets you steam food and keep it moist, or alternatively you can tightly cover the pan with aluminum foil. Skillets have shallower sides and are best used when you really want to brown something over an intensive heat, such as a steak.

Baking and roasting pans: Some of the simplest one-pan dishes are cooked in the oven, so after a little prep work your job is done. A simple ceramic ovenproof dish works well and many of these are elegant enough to bring to table. A sturdy, metal roasting pan is also useful. Try looking for versions with a handle, which makes them easier to get out of the oven. To make sure your food gets browned in the oven, choose a pan that is shallow, otherwise the ingredients will simply steam.

Grill pan: A ridged grill pan will bring all the great taste of an outdoor barbecue inside to your kitchen. The metal dish can be heated on the stove and the ridges will give your food that special seared look. Cooking like this can be smoky, so it's worth having an extractor fan on. It's also a healthy way to cook food. Don't add oil to the pan, rub a little oil over the surface of the food instead, then season and add to the pan. A pair of metal tongs will help you to turn over the food when it's ready. Only robust types of vegetables and meat can be grilled, otherwise they have a tendency to fall apart.

Wok: A mainstay of Asian cooking, woks are great all-around cooking utensils. You can cook large-portion meals in a wok, but make sure not to overcrowd the pan when stir-frying. Cut all the vegetables and meat to the same size so they cook quickly and evenly. Add items such as noodles and rice at the end to get the maximum flavor. You can also use a wok for deep-fat frying, simmering, and steaming, if it has a lid. Heavy woks are a good investment because they will ensure food doesn't burn, but nonstick versions are also available. For a gas flame, look for woks with a round bottom, but for electric or induction hobs, go for a wok with a flat bottom so it won't tip over during cooking.

Using the Best Ingredients

Meat: Many one-pot dishes use slower-cooking cuts taken from the shoulder or leg of the animal. These are tougher cuts and require a long and low simmering in the pot to produce tender meat. When time is of the essence, you need to use quicker-cooking cuts, such as loin. Taken from the middle of the animal, these cuts need to be cooked fast—if you leave them for a long time, they toughen up and tend to dry out.

Precooked vegetables: When you're in a hurry and want to use only one dish, there are plenty of items you should have stocked on your shelves. Preroasted vegetables are available, and some grilled eggplants or zucchini will really lift a dish and save you plenty of time and effort. They are also good to toss in a salad or finely chop to make a simple dressing or sauce.

Canned beans: Dried beans take a long time to cook from scratch, but are perfect for absorbing delicious flavors in a dish as well as being filling. Luckily, you can find most beans canned, and they are simple to drain and then wash before using. As well as being a great addition to dishes, beans make a quick and easy accompaniment—drain and pour over boiling water, then place in a processor and blend until smooth and you'll have an instant mashed bean. You can find lentils in cans, but they are also available in microwavable pouches, which are quick to heat up.

Precooked rice and noodles: You can now buy precooked rice and noodles that are simple to make into a quick one-pot dinner. Cooked rice can be added or simply microwaved in the package, while there is a large selection of noodles available to brighten up a stir-fry. Couscous, a small grain from North Africa, is the perfect quick-cooking ingredient. Measure out a mugful, add to a pan of seared meat or vegetables, then add 1½ mugfuls of boiling stock and cover. A couple of minutes later you'll have fluffy, tender couscous to enjoy.

Prepared pastry: A crisp, rich topping of pastry makes any dinner that bit more special. Store-bought rolled dough pie crusts are available as is ready-to-bake puff pastry. Look for pastry made with butter: it costs a little more, but the flavor is fantastic. In addition to puff pastry and pie crusts, try using phyllo pastry. These thin sheets, which crisp up in the oven, just need brushing over with melted butter or oil and can then be used to make either savory or sweet dishes.

The Finishing Touches

One-pot dishes need to be packed full of flavor, so stock up on some ingredients that will give your meals a sparkling finish.

Herbs: A handful of fresh herbs is an easy way to add fresh flavor and color to the pot. Fresh cilantro leaves will perk up store-bought curry paste, and while fresh pesto is available in stores, you can make your own and experiment with adding lemon juice or capers for an extra kick, or ground almonds and roasted red peppers for a Spanish-inspired taste.

Spices: Spices need a delicate touch—you don't want them to overwhelm a dish, but a pinch of something can make the most mundane meal special. Paprika and dried chile will warm up a dish, while cumin and coriander are essential to many Asian recipes. Cinnamon is versatile and is used in many savory dishes as well as crisps and other desserts.

Cheese: A rich, strong cheese sprinkled over a dish will also help to bring it together. Feta is great for adding flavor to Greek and Mediterranean dishes, while goat cheese also provides a nice tang. Mozzarella melts into just about any dish and sets off the sharpness of tomatoes, while a sprinkling of Parmesan lifts any Italian-inspired dinner.

Serve Alongside

Using just one pot makes life in the kitchen much simpler, but it's easy to also add side dishes without creating more stress. Bread is great with most meals. Choose a dinner roll or baguette to mop up a soupy stew, or crisp up some sliced ciabatta or bake some garlic bread to serve alongside broiled meals or Italian meals. Salads and Mediterranean dishes are perfect with some lightly toasted pita bread.

In the warmer months, whip up a salad to enjoy with your meal. Simply whisk together one part of vinegar or lemon juice with three parts of oil and a pinch of salt, then toss together with a bag of mixed salad greens. You can try different flavors—add a touch of mustard, some chopped herbs, or a flavored vinegar or oil if you prefer something a little different.

Hot and Spicy

Be generous with the spices if you like your food to have that little extra kick

Chicken Pad Thai 28

Tandoori Chicken with Onions and Tomatoes 34

Chicken and Coconut Thai Curry Rice 38

Massaman Chicken Curry with Peanuts 42

Steamed Soy Chicken with Mixed Mushrooms 60

Indian-Style Chicken and Peppers 62

Spicy Salmon with Couscous 94

Fish, Coconut, and Potato Curry 106

Thai Beef Salad with Herbs 130

Sweet Potato and Coconut Curry 182

Corn, Coconut, and Tomato Curry 192

Cinnamon-Spiced Cherries 240

Entertaining

Impress your guests with these delicious main meals and desserts

Chicken, Olive, and Cumin Couscous 50

Seared Duck and Figs with Watercress Salad 68

Herb-Roasted Turkey Breast with Prosciutto and Beans 70

Sea Bass with Herb and Olive Couscous 104

Baked Prosciutto-Wrapped Monkfish with Tapenade 108

Hashed Browns with Smoked Salmon and Arugula 122

Rosemary-Crusted Roasted Lamb 162

Squash with Stilton Fondue 190

Crunchy Berry Brûlée 232

Boozy Caramelized Oranges 256

Tiramisu 258

Vanilla Zabaglione 278

Family Classics

A selection of recipes to please even the fussiest of young eaters

**Melted Cheesy Chicken
Tortilla Wedges** 58

**Oven-Baked Fish and Chips
with Tomato Salsa** 114

**Roasted Sausages with
Parsnips and Carrots** 128

**Melting Meatball
Sandwiches** 134

**Herbed Steak
Tortilla Wraps** 158

**Italian Hamburgers with
Polenta Fries** 164

**Fried Cheese and Zucchini
with Red Pepper Salsa** 196

Pizza Fiorentina 210

**Chocolate Fudge
Brownie Cake** 242

**Choc-Chip Ice Cream
Sandwiches** 250

**Peach and Raspberry
Melba** 264

**Banana and Caramel
Puffs** 270

Soups and Stews

The ultimate one-pot meal, a warming bowl of soup or stew is always welcome

Spicy Chicken Soup
with Avocado 26

French-Style Chicken Stew
with Tarragon 36

Paella Soup 46

Chili Chicken Noodle Soup 54

Spanish Monkfish and
Clam Stew 80

Spicy Fish and Potato Soup 88

Clam, Kale, and Lima Bean
Stew 92

Thai Hot-and-Sour Shrimp
Soup 98

Chorizo and Black Bean
Soup 148

Moroccan Lamb Stew 156

Spicy Beef and Tomato Stew
with Corn 170

Pork and Paprika Goulash 172

Pasta and Noodles

Versatile, quick, and popular—there's a pasta recipe to suit every taste and occasion

Sticky Lemon Chicken Noodles 32

Linguine with Creamy Chicken Carbonara 66

Chile Shrimp Noodles 86

Smoked Haddock and Watercress Cannelloni 110

Shrimp Salad with Peanut Sauce 116

Spicy Seafood Pasta with Garlic Mayonnaise 118

Lamb Stew with Feta and Pasta 142

Stir-Fried Teriyaki Beef with Noodles and Greens 146

Creamy Ham and Tomato Penne 152

Thai Mixed Vegetable Soup 202

Red Pepper and Goat Cheese Lasagne 204

Wintery Minestrone with Pasta and Beans 220

Pies and Tarts

A savory pie or sweet tart makes a wonderful centerpiece for any meal

Chicken and Tomato Polenta Pie 30

Chicken and Ham Pie with Biscuit Topping 48

Phyllo-Topped Chicken, Mushroom, and Dill Pie 56

Crispy Fish Pie 82

Bacon and Apple Puffs 140

Prosciutto and Asparagus Tart 144

Crispy Spinach and Feta Pie 180

Tomato and Basil Tart 184

Pastry-Topped Summer Vegetables 214

Apple and Orange Tart 234

Prune Clafoutis 260

Apricot and Almond Crostata 266

Winter Warmers

Hearty, wholesome fare to warm you up on a chilly winter's night

Cod with Creamy Chowder Sauce 120

Beef Stew with Garlic Bread Topping 138

Sausage and Bean Cassoulet 160

Sweet Potato and Chorizo Hash 174

Beet Risotto with Goat Cheese 198

Cauliflower with Leeks and Cheese Sauce 212

Tomato and Eggplant Pilaf 216

Baked Zucchini and Ricotta 222

Rhubarb and Ginger Slump 248

Baked Figs with Honey and Pistachios 252

Creamy Chocolate Puddings 268

Crunchy Pear Crisp 276

Summer Favorites

These fresh, light dishes are perfect for a sunny summer's day

Chicken with Warm Lentils and Kale 52

Rice with Salmon and Lemon Dressing 76

Shrimp and Pea Risotto 78

Steamed Lemon Dill Salmon and Potatoes 84

Seared Tuna with Lemon, Bean, and Arugula Salad 112

Herbed Pork and Lentil Salad 168

Pea and Asparagus Risotto 194

Feta-Stuffed Roasted Peppers 200

Tortilla with Tomato and Arugula Salad 224

Strawberry Cream Puffs 236

Tropical Fruit Salad 244

Lemon Syllabub 274

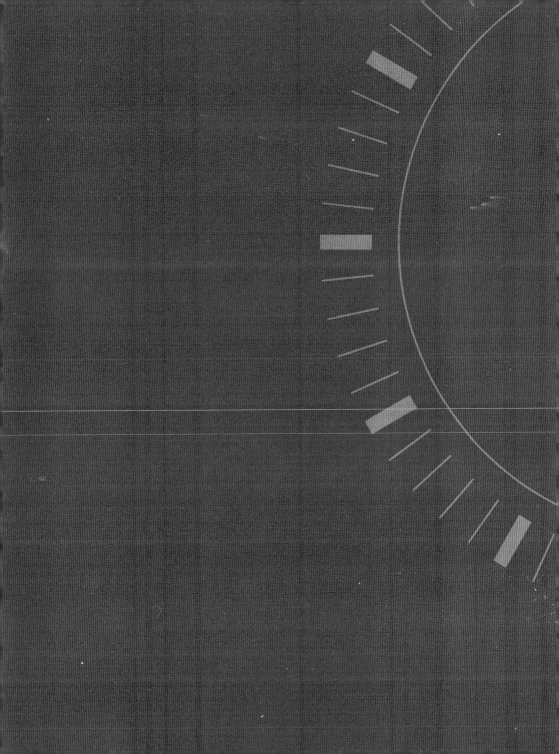

QuickCook
Poultry

Recipes listed by cooking time

10

30 Roasted Chicken with Butternut Squash

Serves 4

½ lb butternut squash, peeled and
cut into thin slices
1 red onion, sliced
4 bone-in chicken breasts
2 tablespoons olive oil
1 tablespoon balsamic vinegar
¼ cup walnut halves
8 sage leaves
salt and black pepper

To serve

crusty bread
green salad

- Arrange the squash, onion, and chicken, skin side up, in a roasting pan.

- Drizzle with the oil, season to taste, and toss to make sure everything is well coated in oil. Place in a preheated oven, at 400°F, for 15 minutes.

- Drizzle with the balsamic vinegar and sprinkle the walnuts and sage leaves around the chicken. Return to the oven for 5–10 minutes, until the squash is tender and the chicken is cooked through. Serve with crusty bread and green salad.

---

10 Chicken, Butternut, and Goat Cheese Pasta Cook 1¾ cups peeled and diced butternut squash in a large saucepan of lightly salted boiling water for 6 minutes. Add 1 lb fresh penne pasta and cook for another 3 minutes, or according to the package directions, until "al dente." Add 1 (5 oz) package baby spinach leaves, then drain immediately and return the pasta and vegetables to the pan. Stir in ⅓ cup soft goat cheese and 1 cooked chicken breast, torn into shreds, then season to taste and serve topped with coarsely chopped walnuts.

20 Chicken, Butternut, and Bean Stew Heat 2 tablespoons vegetable oil in a shallow, flameproof casserole dish. Add 2 cups peeled and diced butternut squash and 10 oz diced chicken breast. Season to taste and cook for 5 minutes, until golden. Add 2 crushed garlic cloves, 2 finely chopped sage leaves, and 1 cup hot chicken stock and bring to a boil. Reduce the heat and simmer for 12 minutes or until the chicken and squash are cooked through. Add a 1 cup rinsed and drained, canned cannellini beans, then cook for another 2 minutes, until heated through. Sprinkle with chopped parsley to serve.

 # Spicy Chicken Soup with Avocado

Serves 4

2 tablespoons olive oil
1 onion, chopped
3 garlic cloves, crushed
1 teaspoon chipotle peppers in adobo sauce, chopped, or Tabasco sauce
2 teaspoons sugar
1 (14½ oz) can diced tomatoes
4 cups hot chicken stock
2 cooked chicken breasts, torn into strips
1 avocado, peeled, pitted, and cubed
handful of tortilla chips, crushed
¼ cup sour cream
handful of chopped fresh cilantro
salt and black pepper

- Heat the oil in a large saucepan. Add the onion and cook for 5 minutes, until softened, then stir in the garlic, chipotle or Tabasco, and sugar. Pour in the tomatoes and stock, bring to a boil, then reduce the heat and simmer for 10 minutes.

- Use a handheld electric blender to puree the soup until smooth, then add a little boiling water if it is too thick and season to taste.

- Ladle the soup into bowls and sprinkle the chicken, avocado, and tortilla chips on top. Top with the sour cream and sprinkle with the cilantro.

 Spicy Chicken and Avocado Salad

Mix a few drops of Tabasco sauce with ½ teaspoon ground cumin and 1 tablespoon olive oil. Coat 2 chicken breasts, cut into strips, in the oil. Cook in a hot grill pan for 3 minutes on each side or until cooked through. Toss together 4 cups mixed salad greens, 2 chopped tomatoes, 1 sliced avocado, the chicken, some crushed tortilla chips, the juice of ½ lime, and 1 tablespoon olive oil.

Broiled Spicy Chicken Wings with Tomato and Avocado Salsa Mix together 1 teaspoon honey, 1 teaspoon tomato paste, ½ teaspoon ground cumin, ½ finely chopped red chile, 1 tablespoon olive oil, and 1 tablespoon lime juice in a large bowl. Season to taste, add 12 chicken wings, toss to coat, and let marinate for 10 minutes. Cook the wings under a preheated hot broiler for 5–6 minutes on each side until golden and cooked through. Coarsely chop 2 avocados and 1 tomato and mix together with 1 sliced scallion, 1 tablespoon olive oil, 1 tablespoon lime juice, and a large handful of chopped fresh cilantro. Season to taste and serve the salad with the hot chicken wings.

10 Chicken Pad Thai

Serves 4

3 tablespoons vegetable oil
1 egg, lightly beaten
1 garlic clove, crushed
2 teaspoons finely grated fresh
ginger root
2 scallions, sliced
4 oz rice noodles, cooked
½ cup bean sprouts
2 cooked chicken breasts, torn
into thin strips
2 tablespoons Thai fish sauce
2 teaspoons tamarind paste
2 teaspoons sugar
pinch of chili powder
¼ cup roasted coarsely chopped
peanuts
handful of chopped fresh cilantro

- Heat a large wok or skillet until smoking hot. Add 1 tablespoon of the oil and swirl around the wok, then pour in the egg. Stir around the wok and cook for 1–2 minutes, until just cooked through. Remove from the wok and set aside.

- Heat the remaining oil in the wok, add the garlic, ginger, and scallions, and cook for 2 minutes, until softened. Add the noodles to the wok along with the bean sprouts and chicken.

- Stir in the fish sauce, tamarind paste, sugar, and chili powder and continue to cook, adding a splash of boiling water, if necessary. Heat through, then return the egg to the wok and mix in. Divide among serving bowls and sprinkle with the peanuts and cilantro to serve.

20 Broiled Chicken Noodle Salad

Prepare 8 oz dried rice noodles according to the package directions. Meanwhile, mix 2 tablespoons sweet chili sauce with 2 tablespoons lime juice and brush over 2 skinless chicken breasts. Cook under a preheated medium broiler for 5 minutes, turn over, and cook for another 5–7 minutes, until cooked through, then slice thickly. Drain the noodles, cool under cold running water, if necessary, and drain again. Mix 1 teaspoon granulated sugar, 2 tablespoons rice vinegar, and 2 teaspoons Thai fish sauce and stir into the noodles with the chicken, 1 shredded carrot, ¼ finely chopped cucumber, and a large handful each of chopped fresh cilantro and mint. Sprinkle with sesame seeds to serve.

30 Chicken Noodle Soup

Simmer 5 cups chicken stock with 3 tablespoons rice wine, 2 tablespoons light soy sauce, and 1 star anise for 10 minutes. Mix 10 oz ground chicken with 1 teaspoon grated fresh ginger root and 1 teaspoon soy sauce. Shape into balls and cook in the soup for 7 minutes. Add 4 oz shiitake mushrooms and cook for another 3 minutes. Stir in 2 bok choy, quartered, and cook for 1 minute. Add 4 oz rice noodles, cooked, heat through, and serve.

ONE-POUL-MYN

30 Chicken and Tomato Polenta Pie

Serves 4

2 tablespoons olive oil

10 oz skinless chicken breasts, diced

2 garlic cloves, finely chopped

1 teaspoon tomato paste

1 (14½ oz) can diced tomatoes

pinch of dried red pepper flakes

handful of chopped basil

1 zucchini, sliced

1 lb Italian-style polenta log, cut into ½ inch slices

¼ cup grated Parmesan cheese

salt and black pepper

- Heat the oil in a shallow, flameproof casserole dish. Add the chicken, season to taste, and cook for 3–4 minutes until starting to turn golden, then remove from the dish and set aside.

- Add the garlic to the dish, cook for 1 minute, then pour in the tomatoes. Stir in the red pepper flakes and basil, bring to a boil, then reduce the heat and simmer for 10 minutes.

- Return the chicken to the dish along with the zucchini and cook for another 5–10 minutes, until the chicken is just cooked through.

- Arrange the polenta slices on top of the chicken mixture, then sprinkle with the Parmesan. Cook under a preheated hot broiler for 5 minutes or until golden and bubbling.

 Corn, Tomato, and Chicken Salad Heat 1 tablespoon olive oil in a skillet. Add ½ cup fresh or canned corn kernels and cook for 3 minutes, until browned. Chop 1 romaine lettuce and toss with 2 chopped tomatoes and 2 cooked chicken breasts, torn into shreds. Mix ¼ cup buttermilk with 1 teaspoon cider vinegar and 1 teaspoon sugar and season to taste. Sprinkle the corn over the salad, then drizzle with the buttermilk dressing and serve immediately.

 Grilled Polenta with Chicken and Tomatoes Heat a grill pan until smoking hot. Rub 1 tablespoon olive oil over 4 boneless, skinless chicken breasts. Season to taste and cook for 5–7 minutes on each side until just cooked through. Cut into thick slices and toss with 4 chopped tomatoes, 1 tablespoon sherry vinegar, 3 tablespoons extra virgin olive oil, and a large handful of chopped fresh basil. Cut 1 lb Italian-style polenta log into thick slices. Brush a little oil on each slice, then cook in the grill pan for 2 minutes on each side until charred. Spoon the warm chicken mixture over the polenta to serve.

ONE-POUL-BIE

10 Sticky Lemon Chicken Noodles

Serves 4

2 tablespoons vegetable oil

10 oz chicken breasts, cut into thin strips

8 oz baby broccoli

2 garlic cloves, crushed

2 teaspoons finely grated fresh ginger root

1 red chile, finely chopped

finely grated rind and juice of 1 lemon

1 tablespoon honey

2 teaspoons light soy sauce

4 oz egg noodles, cooked

handful of roasted cashew nuts

- Heat a wok or large skillet until smoking hot, then pour in the oil, swirl around the wok, and add the chicken. Cook for 1 minute, then add the broccoli and cook for 5 minutes, until the chicken is nearly cooked through.

- Add the garlic, ginger, and chile to the wok and cook for another 1 minute. Then add the lemon rind and juice, the honey, and soy sauce and toss around the wok.

- Add the noodles and a splash of water and cook until heated through. Divide among serving bowls, sprinkle with the cashew nuts, and serve.

20 Roasted Lemon Chicken with Broccoli

Mix together 1 teaspoon ground cumin, 1 teaspoon honey, 1 crushed garlic clove, and 3 tablespoons olive oil. Stir in the finely grated rind of 1 lemon and a squeeze of lemon juice and season to taste. Place 4 chicken breasts and 8 oz baby broccoli in a roasting pan. Pour the lemon mixture over the top and toss well. Place in a preheated oven, at 400°F, for 15 minutes or until the chicken is cooked through. Sprinkle with some sesame seeds and serve with boiled rice.

30 Lemon Chicken Risotto

Heat 1 tablespoon olive oil in a large saucepan. Add 1 finely chopped shallot and 1 crushed garlic clove and cook for 5 minutes, until softened. Stir in 1¾ cup risotto rice followed by ½ cup dry white wine and let simmer until boiled away. Gradually add 4 cups hot chicken stock, a ladleful at a time, stirring continuously and letting each ladleful be absorbed before adding the next. After 15 minutes, add 2 cooked chicken breasts, torn into strips. Stir in the finely grated rind of 1 lemon and cook for another 2 minutes or until the rice is tender, then add a squeeze of lemon juice. Season to taste and spoon into serving bowls, then spoon ⅓ cup mascarpone cheese on top and add a handful of arugula to each portion.

ONE-POUL-JOE

 # Tandoori Chicken with Onions and Tomatoes

Serves 4

4 skinless chicken breasts
½ cup plain yogurt
1 garlic clove, crushed
2 teaspoons finely grated
   fresh ginger root
2 tablespoons tandoori
   curry paste
1 onion, cut into wedges
2 tablespoons vegetable oil
2 tomatoes, quartered
1 tablespoon butter, cut into
   small pieces
salt and black pepper

To serve

lime wedges
store-bought raita
naans

- Line a baking sheet with aluminum foil and set a wire rack on top. Make 3 slashes across each chicken breast. Mix together the yogurt, garlic, ginger, and tandoori paste and season well. Rub all over the chicken and let marinate for 5–10 minutes.

- Toss the onion and chicken with the oil, then arrange on the rack. Place in a preheated oven, at 450°F, for 7 minutes.

- Add the tomatoes, dot with the butter, and return to the oven for another 5–10 minutes, until the chicken is browned and cooked through. Serve with lime wedges, raita, and naan.

Easy Tandoori Chicken Curry

Heat 1 tablespoon vegetable oil in a large, heavy saucepan. Add 1 crushed garlic clove and 1 teaspoon finely grated fresh ginger root and cook for 1 minute, then stir in 2 teaspoons tomato paste and 1 tablespoon curry powder. Add ¾ cup canned diced tomatoes and simmer for 5 minutes. Add 12 oz cooked tandoori chicken breasts, cut into strips, and ¼ cup heavy cream. Heat until piping hot, then serve with naan.

 ### Tandoori Chicken Skewers

Cut 12 oz boneless, skinless chicken thighs into chunks. Mix ¼ cup plain yogurt with 1 teaspoon paprika, 1 teaspoon ground cumin, and ½ teaspoon ground coriander. Add a squeeze of lemon juice, then use to coat the chicken chunks. Thread the chicken onto metal skewers, alternating with onion wedges and cherry tomatoes. Heat a grill pan until smoking hot, brush 1 tablespoon oil over the skewers, then cook for 5–7 minutes on each side until browned and cooked through. Sprinkle with chopped fresh cilantro and serve on warm Indian-style bread.

French-Style Chicken Stew with Tarragon

Serves 4

1 leek, sliced
4 boneless, skinless chicken
   thighs, cut into chunks
12 oz small new potatoes, halved
1 carrot, sliced
1¾ cups hot chicken stock
¼ cup dry white wine
⅔ cup frozen peas, defrosted
2 tablespoons crème fraîche or
   sour cream
salt and black pepper
handful of chopped tarragon,
   to serve

- Place the leek, chicken, potatoes, and carrot in a large saucepan. Pour in the stock and wine and season to taste.

- Bring to a boil, then reduce the heat and simmer for 15 minutes, until just cooked through.

- Stir in the peas and crème fraîche or sour cream and heat through. Sprinkle with the tarragon and serve immediately.

 Chicken Sauté with Peas, Lettuce, and Tarragon Heat 1 tablespoon oil in a saucepan. Add 10 oz thinly sliced chicken and cook for 2 minutes, until golden. Add 1 crushed garlic clove and cook for another 30 seconds. Pour in 2 tablespoons dry white wine and simmer for 1 minute, then add ¼ cup chicken stock and boil hard for 2 minutes. Stir in ⅔ cup defrosted frozen peas, 1 sliced Boston lettuce, and 2 tablespoons crème fraîche or sour cream, season to taste, and heat through. Sprinkle with chopped tarragon and serve with toasted baguette slices.

 Steamed Tarragon Chicken Packages Cut 4 large squares of nonstick parchment paper. Place 1 small skinless chicken breast fillet on each. Divide 4 thickly sliced baby leeks and 8 baby carrots, halved lengthwise, among the packages and place a slice of butter and a sprig of tarragon on top of each chicken breast. Season to taste, fold the paper over, and roll up the edges to create airtight packages, leaving just a little gap. Pour 2 tablespoons dry white wine into each package and then fully seal, leaving enough space in the packages for air to circulate.

Place on a baking sheet and cook in a preheated oven, at 425°F, for 20 minutes or until cooked through. Serve with boiled rice, if desired.

30 Chicken and Coconut Thai Curry Rice

Serves 4

1 tablespoon vegetable oil

1 onion, finely chopped

1 garlic clove, crushed

2 teaspoons finely grated fresh
ginger root

2 tablespoons Thai green curry
paste

12 oz thick chicken breast strips

1 red bell pepper, cored, seeded,
and thickly sliced

1⅓ cups jasmine rice

1¾ cups coconut milk

1½ cups chicken stock

salt and black pepper

chopped basil, to garnish

lime wedges, to serve

- Heat the oil in a large, flameproof casserole dish or heavy saucepan. Add the onion and cook for 5 minutes, until softened. Stir in the garlic, ginger, and curry paste and cook for another 1 minute. Add the chicken and red bell pepper, followed by the rice, and stir well.

- Pour in the coconut milk and stock and season to taste. Bring to a boil, then reduce the heat and simmer for about 10 minutes, until nearly all the liquid has boiled away.

- Turn the heat down as low as it will go, cover the dish, and cook for another 5 minutes or until the rice is cooked through. Sprinkle with the basil and serve the rice hot with lime wedges for squeezing.

 Stir-Fried Thai Chicken with Coconut Milk Heat a wok, then add 2 tablespoons vegetable oil. Add 1 sliced shallot and cook for 1 minute, then add 12 oz chicken breast cut into thick strips. Stir-fry for 5 minutes, until the chicken is nearly cooked through. Add 1 crushed garlic clove and 1 teaspoon finely grated fresh ginger root and cook for 1 minute. Add 2 tablespoons Thai fish sauce, 2 teaspoons sugar, 6 cherry tomatoes, and ½ cup coconut milk and simmer for 1 minute until the chicken is cooked through. Serve with rice noodles.

 Spicy Coconut and Chicken Soup Heat 1 tablespoon oil in a large, heavy saucepan. Add 2 finely chopped shallots and cook for 2 minutes to soften. Stir in 2 teaspoons finely grated fresh ginger root and 2 tablespoons Thai green curry paste. Cook for another 1 minute, then add 1¾ cups coconut milk, 4 cups hot chicken stock, 2 tablespoons Thai fish sauce, 2 teaspoons sugar, 1 lemon grass stalk, and 2 kaffir lime leaves. Bring to a boil, then reduce the heat and simmer for 10 minutes. Stir in 2 cooked chicken breasts, torn into shreds, 4 oz rice noodles, cooked, and 1 cup drained, canned bamboo shoots and simmer until heated through. Ladle into bowls and serve sprinkled with bean sprouts, finely chopped red chile, and fresh cilantro leaves.

 # Chicken Breasts with Mascarpone Cheese and Tomatoes

Serves 4

3 tablespoons olive oil,
  plus extra for greasing
¼ cup mascarpone cheese
4 teaspoons fresh green pesto
4 skinless chicken breasts
1 cup dried bread crumbs
8 cherry tomatoes
3 tablespoons toasted pine nuts
salt and black pepper
crusty bread, to serve (optional)

- Mix together the mascarpone and pesto. Use a small, sharp knife to make a horizontal slit in the side of each chicken breast to form a pocket. Fill the pockets with the mascarpone mixture.

- Season the chicken and rub with 1 tablespoon of the oil then turn in the bread crumbs until well coated. Place in a baking sheet, drizzle with another tablespoon of oil, and cook in a preheated oven, at 400°F, for 10 minutes.

- Add the tomatoes to the baking sheet, season, and drizzle with the remaining oil. Return to the oven for another 5 minutes or until the chicken is cooked through. Sprinkle with the pine nuts and serve with crusty bread, if desired.

---

10 Chicken Pizza Melts with Cheese and Tomatoes Cut 2 skinless chicken breasts in half horizontally and place on a lightly greased baking sheet. Top each with a slice of tomato and a slice of mozzarella cheese, then season to taste. Cook under a preheated hot broiler for 7 minutes or until the cheese has melted and the chicken is cooked through. Serve in burger buns with a few salad greens.

30 Roasted Chicken with Goat Cheese and Tomatoes Ease the skin away from 4 bone-in chicken breasts to create a small pocket, making sure the skin is still attached on 3 sides. Cut 3 oz soft goat cheese into 4 thick slices. Tuck a slice of cheese under the skin of each chicken breast and top with a sprig of thyme. Place in a lightly greased large roasting pan with 4 unpeeled garlic cloves.

Place in a preheated oven, at 400°F, for 15 minutes. Remove the garlic cloves and squeeze out the flesh. Add 1 (14½ oz) can diced tomatoes to the pan, stir in the garlic, and season well. Return to the oven for another 5 minutes, then add 1 (14 oz) can cannellini beans, rinsed and drained. Cook for another 3–5 minutes, until the beans are hot and the chicken is cooked through, then serve.

3⦿ Chicken Curry with Peanuts

Serves 4

1 tablespoon vegetable oil

4 boneless, skinless chicken thighs, cut into chunks

2 tablespoons curry paste

3 tablespoons smooth peanut butter

⅔ cup coconut milk

⅔ cup chicken stock

1 lemon grass stalk

1 tablespoon Thai fish sauce

2 teaspoons packed brown sugar

2 large waxy potatoes, peeled and cut into chunks

salt and black pepper

handful of chopped fresh cilantro

handful of roasted peanuts, coarsely chopped

- Heat the oil in a large saucepan or wok. Add the chicken and cook for 7 minutes, until golden. Add the curry paste and stir to coat. Stir in the peanut butter, coconut milk, and stock, season to taste, and stir well.

- Add the lemon grass, fish sauce, sugar, and potatoes, bring to a boil, then reduce the heat and simmer for 15 minutes or until the chicken and potatoes are cooked through. Spoon into bowls, sprinkle with the cilantro and peanuts and serve hot.

1⦿ Stir-Fried Chicken with Peanuts

Heat 1 tablespoon vegetable oil in a wok. Add 2 tablespoons raw peanuts and cook for 2 minutes. Remove from the pan and add 1 sliced shallot and 10 oz sliced chicken breast. Stir-fry for 2 minutes, then add 1 crushed garlic clove, 1 teaspoon grated fresh ginger root, and 6 halved cherry tomatoes. Toss, then add 1 tablespoon Thai fish sauce, 1 teaspoon sugar, and 4 oz rice noodles, cooked. Stir well, then add the peanuts and a squeeze of lime.

2⦿ Peanut and Chicken Thighs

Brush 1 tablespoon vegetable oil and 1 teaspoon curry paste over 4 boneless, skinless chicken thighs. Place on a baking sheet and cook in a preheated oven, at 400°F, for 10 minutes. Mix 2 teaspoons curry paste with ⅓ cup peanut butter and 3 tablespoons coconut milk or water. Drizzle 2 tablespoons of the mixture over the chicken and return to the oven for another 5 minutes or until the chicken is cooked through. Place the remaining sauce in a dipping bowl and serve with the chicken, with slices of cucumber, plenty of shrimp crackers, and boiled rice, if desired.

2⊘ Citrus-Grilled Chicken with Hummus and Pita

Serves 4

2 teaspoons ground sumac (optional)

handful of thyme leaves, finely chopped

finely grated rind and juice of 1 lemon

1½ tablespoons olive oil

4 boneless, skinless chicken thighs

4 pita breads

salt and black pepper

To serve

arugula leaves

store-bought hummus

- Mix the sumac, thyme, and grated lemon rind with the olive oil. Season to taste, then rub all over the chicken and set aside for 5 minutes.

- Heat a ridged grill pan until smoking hot. Cook the pita breads for 1–2 minutes on each side until lightly browned, then set aside.

- Cook the chicken thighs for 4–5 minutes on each side until lightly browned and cooked through. Squeeze a little lemon juice over the arugula and divide among serving plates. Cut the chicken into pieces and arrange on the plates with a spoonful of hummus and the pita breads, torn into strips.

 Seared Chicken with Chickpeas and Pita Breads Heat 1 tablespoon olive oil in a skillet. Add 10 oz diced chicken breast and cook for 5 minutes, until golden. Stir in 1 finely chopped garlic clove and 1 teaspoon ground cumin. Add 1 (15 oz) can chickpeas, rinsed and drained, to the pan along with ¼ cup chicken stock. Season to taste and simmer for 3–4 minutes, until the chicken is cooked through. Sprinkle with 1 teaspoon ground sumac and a handful of chopped parsley, then serve with warm pita breads.

 Hummus-Crumbed Chicken in Pita Pockets Spread ½ cup hummus over 4 skinless chicken breasts. Place 1 cup dried bread crumbs on a plate. Mix in the finely grated rind of 1 lemon and 1 teaspoon ground sumac. Roll the chicken in the bread crumbs until well coated. Place on a baking sheet and drizzle with 2 tablespoons olive oil. Place in a preheated oven, at 400°F, for 15 minutes or until cooked through. Cut the chicken into slices and serve inside pita breads with some tomato slices and arugula.

2🕐 Paella Soup

Serves 4

1 tablespoon olive oil
1 onion, finely chopped
8 oz chorizo, chopped
2 garlic cloves, crushed
¾ cup can diced tomatoes
4 cups chicken stock
pinch of saffron threads
2 skinless chicken breasts, cubed
1 red bell pepper, cored, seeded,
  and chopped
2 cups cooked rice
⅓ cup frozen peas, defrosted
salt and black pepper

- Heat the oil in a large, heavy saucepan. Add the onion and chorizo and cook for 2 minutes or until the onion has softened and the chorizo is lightly browned.

- Stir in the garlic, then add the tomatoes, stock, and saffron, and season to taste. Bring to a boil, add the chicken and red pepper, and simmer for 10–12 minutes or until the chicken is cooked through.

- Add the rice and peas and cook for 2–3 minutes, until heated through. Ladle the soup into bowls and serve.

 Chicken, Chorizo, and Tomato Skewers Toss 10 oz diced, skinless chicken breasts and 6 cherry tomatoes in 2 tablespoons olive oil and season well. Cut 8 oz chorizo into thick slices. Thread the chicken, tomatoes, and chorizo onto metal skewers and cook under a preheated hot broiler for 3–5 minutes on each side or until cooked through. Serve in lightly toasted baguettes with a handful of arugula.

3🕐 **Chicken, Chorizo, and Shrimp Paella** Heat 1 tablespoon oil in a skillet. Add 8 oz chopped chorizo and cook for 3 minutes, until browned, then remove from the skillet and set aside. Add 1 finely chopped onion and 4 diced boneless, skinless chicken thighs to the skillet and cook for 2 minutes. Stir in 2 crushed garlic cloves and 1⅓ cups paella or Spanish rice. Add 1 cored, seeded, and sliced green bell pepper and the chorizo. Pour in 3 cups chicken stock and a pinch of saffron threads and cook for 10 minutes. Stir in 4 oz large, peeled shrimp and cook for another 5–10 minutes, until the rice is tender and the shrimp are cooked through. Serve sprinkled with chopped parsley.

30 Chicken and Ham Pie with Biscuit Topping

Serves 4

2 tablespoons butter

2 leeks, sliced

10 oz skinless, boneless chicken thighs, diced

5 oz piece of ham, cut into small chunks

⅔ cup hot chicken stock

½ cup crème fraîche or heavy cream

1¼ cups all-purpose flour

1 tablespoon baking powder

2 tablespoons olive oil

⅔ cup milk

2 tablespoons mixed herbs (such as parsley, thyme, chives), finely chopped

¼ cup shredded cheddar cheese

salt and black pepper

- Melt the butter in a shallow, flameproof casserole dish. Add the leeks and cook for 3 minutes, until softened. Add the chicken and cook for 2 minutes, until lightly browned all over. Stir in the ham, stock, and crème fraîche or heavy cream, then season to taste.

- Mix the flour and baking powder in a bowl, then pour in the oil and milk. Mix gently, season well, and stir in the herbs and cheese.

- Arrange spoonfuls of the dough on top of the chicken mixture, leaving a little space between each spoonful. Place in a preheated oven, at 425°F, for 15–20 minutes, until the topping is lightly browned and the chicken is cooked through.

10 Creamy Chicken and Ham Pasta

Cook 12 oz quick-cook spaghetti in a large saucepan of lightly salted boiling water according to the package directions, adding 1 finely sliced leek for the last 5 minutes of cooking. Drain and return the pasta and leek to the pan. Stir in 2 cooked chicken breasts, torn into shreds, and 4 slices of ham, torn into strips. Season well, add ¼ cup crème fraîche or heavy cream, then sprinkle with chopped parsley to serve.

20 Biscuits with Chicken and Ham

Place 2⅔ cups all-purpose flour in a food processor with 6 tablespoons cold butter, cut into cubes, 1 teaspoon baking powder, ⅔ cup buttermilk, and a pinch of salt. Blend until a smooth dough forms. Knead in 2 finely chopped scallions. Turn the dough onto a lightly floured surface and roll out to about ¾ inch thick. Use a 3 inch round cutter to cut out about 8 biscuits, rerolling the scraps to make more biscuits. Place on a floured baking sheet and cook in a preheated oven, at 425°F, for about 12 minutes, until just cooked through. Split the biscuits and place a slice of ham and a slice of cooked chicken inside each. Top with shredded lettuce and a spoonful of mayonnaise.

10 Chicken, Olive, and Cumin Couscous

Serves 4

¼ cup olive oil
½ lemon (rind and flesh),
  finely chopped
1 tablespoon honey
½ teaspoon ground cumin
1 garlic clove, crushed
1½ cups couscous
1¼ cups hot chicken stock
1 (15 oz) can chickpeas, rinsed
  and drained
½ cup green olives, pitted
2 cooked chicken breasts, sliced
handful each of chopped fresh
  cilantro and mint
salt and black pepper

- Heat the oil and lemon in a saucepan and cook over gentle heat for about 2 minutes, until the lemon is soft.

- Stir in the honey, cumin, and garlic and heat through. Stir in the couscous, stock, chickpeas, olives, and chicken.

- Remove from the heat and let rest for 5 minutes, until the couscous is tender. Fluff up with a fork and stir in the cilantro and mint. Season to taste and serve immediately.

20 Cumin-Dusted Chicken Breasts with Spicy Olive Couscous

Heat 2 tablespoons oil in a skillet. Dust 4 small chicken breasts with 1 teaspoon ground cumin, season, and cook for 5 minutes on each side until just cooked through. Stir in 1 crushed garlic clove and 2 teaspoons harissa or chili paste. Add 1¼ cups couscous, 1½ cups hot chicken stock, and ½ cup green olives. Cover and let rest for 5 minutes, until the couscous is tender. Fluff up with a fork and stir in a handful each of chopped mint and fresh cilantro and the grated rind and juice of ½ lemon.

30 Chicken Stewed with Peppers, Olives and Cumin

Mix together 2 tablespoons olive oil, 3 crushed garlic cloves, 1 teaspoon ground cumin, ½ teaspoon ground turmeric, a pinch of chili powder, ¼ cup lemon juice, 2 handfuls of finely chopped fresh cilantro, and a handful of finely chopped parsley. Rub most of the paste over 4 skinless chicken breasts. Heat 2 tablespoons olive oil in a sauté pan or deep skillet with a lid. Add 12 oz sliced new potatoes and cook for 5 minutes, until starting to brown. Stir in the remaining herb paste with 1 cored, seeded, and chopped green bell pepper, then place the chicken on top. Pour in ½ cup chicken stock and cover the pan tightly. Cook over low heat for 20 minutes or until cooked through. Serve with steamed couscous, if desired.

2 ⏱ Chicken with Warm Lentils and Kale

Serves 4

2 tablespoons olive oil

4 skinless chicken breasts

1 garlic clove, sliced

1½ cups chopped kale

1¼ cups rinsed and drained canned green lentils or cooked green lentils

2 tablespoons lemon juice

4 plum or cherry tomatoes

½ cup crumbled soft goat cheese

salt and black pepper

- Heat half the oil in a large skillet. Add the chicken, season to taste, and cook for 5 minutes, then turn over and cook for 2 minutes, until brown all over.

- Add the remaining oil to the skillet along with the garlic, kale, and a splash of water. Cover and cook for 7 minutes, until the kale is tender and the chicken cooked through.

- Stir in the lentils and heat through, then add the lemon juice and tomatoes. Check and adjust the seasoning, if necessary. Cut the chicken into thick slices and arrange on plates with the lentils. Sprinkle with the goat cheese and serve immediately.

 Lentil, Kale, and Chicken Bruschetta

Cook ¾ cup finely chopped kale in a saucepan of lightly salted boiling water for 5–7 minutes, until tender. Add ½ cup rinsed and drained canned green lentils or cooked lentils for the last minute of cooking, then drain well. Spread 3 oz soft goat cheese over 8 thick slices of toasted ciabatta. Mix the warm lentils with 2 teaspoons balsamic vinegar, 2 tablespoons olive oil, and ½ cup chopped sun-dried tomatoes, season to taste, and spoon onto the toasts. Tear 1 cooked chicken breast into strips and arrange on top, then drizzle with 1 tablespoon walnut oil and sprinkle with a handful of toasted walnut halves.

 Hearty Lentil, Kale, and Chicken Soup

Heat 2 tablespoons olive oil in a saucepan. Add 1 finely chopped onion and cook gently for 5 minutes, then add 2 chopped garlic cloves, 1 teaspoon tomato paste, and a pinch of dried red pepper flakes and cook for another 1 minute. Pour in 8 cups chicken stock and bring to a boil. Add 1 cup dried red lentils and simmer for 5 minutes. Skim off any scum that rises to the surface, add 8 oz diced chicken breast, and cook for another 5 minutes. Add 1½ cups chopped kale and simmer for 7 minutes, until tender. Season to taste and serve in warm bowls with crusty bread.

 # Spicy Chicken Noodle Soup

Serves 4

5 cups hot chicken stock
1 tablespoon chili sauce
2 teaspoons Thai fish sauce
1 teaspoon soy sauce
2 teaspoons rice vinegar
2 teaspoons mirin
  (Japanese rice wine)
2 skinless chicken breasts
4 oz ramen or egg noodles,
  cooked
2 bok choy, quartered
¾ cup bean sprouts
1 red chile, sliced
handful of chopped fresh cilantro
lime wedges, to serve

• Pour the stock into a large saucepan, add the chili sauce, fish sauce, soy sauce, rice vinegar, and mirin and bring to a boil. Reduce to a simmer, then add the chicken breasts and cook for 10–15 minutes, until just cooked through. Remove from the pan and cut into thick slices.

• Add the noodles and bok choy to the pan and cook for 2 minutes or until tender and heated through. Ladle the soup into bowls. Arrange the chicken on top, then sprinkle with the bean sprouts, chile, and cilantro and serve with lime wedges.

 Spicy Chicken Soup in a Cup

Heat 2½ cups chicken stock in a saucepan to boiling point. Add 1 teaspoon chili sauce, 2 teaspoons soy sauce, 4 oz egg noodles, cooked, 1 cooked chicken breast, torn into shreds, 2 cups baby spinach leaves, and ½ cup bean sprouts. Divide among large cups and top each serving with a sprinkling of sesame seeds.

 Teriyaki Chicken with Noodles

Mix together ⅓ cup soy sauce, ⅓ cup mirin (Japanese rice wine), 1 tablespoon granulated sugar,1 crushed garlic clove, and 1 teaspoon finely grated fresh ginger root. Add 12 oz diced boneless, skinless chicken thighs, toss to coat, and let marinate for 10 minutes. Heat 3 tablespoons vegetable oil in a wok. Add 1 sliced shallot and stir-fry for 1 minute. Remove the chicken from the marinade, add to the wok, and stir-fry for 5 minutes. Add 1 cored, seeded, and sliced red bell pepper and stir-fry for about another 5 minutes, until the chicken is cooked through. Add 4 oz egg noodles, cooked, ¾ cup bean sprouts and the marinade and heat through until piping hot before serving.

Phyllo-Topped Chicken, Mushroom, and Dill Pie

Serves 4

1 tablespoon vegetable oil
1 onion, finely chopped
10 oz skinless chicken breasts, diced
2½ cups quartered mushrooms
3 tablespoons dry white wine
⅓ cup crème fraîche or heavy cream
finely grated rind of 1 lemon
handful of chopped dill
3 large phyllo pastry sheets
3 tablespoons butter, melted
salt and black pepper

- Heat the oil in a shallow, ovenproof casserole dish. Add the onion and cook for 2 minutes, then stir in the chicken and cook for another 5 minutes. Add the mushrooms and continue to cook for 1 minute, until starting to soften.

- Pour in the wine, cook until it has simmered away, then stir in the crème fraîche or heavy cream, lemon rind, and dill and remove from the heat. Season to taste.

- Meanwhile, unwrap the phyllo pastry and cover with damp paper towels until ready to use it. Working quickly, brush 1 sheet with melted butter and cut into 3 long strips. Arrange the strips on top of the chicken, scrunching it up a little. Repeat with the remaining pastry until the chicken is covered.

- Brush all over with any remaining butter, then place in a preheated oven, at 400°F, for 15–20 minutes, until the phyllo pastry is crisp and the chicken is cooked through.

---

1 **Chicken and Wild Mushrooms in a Creamy Dill Sauce** Heat 1 tablespoon olive oil in a skillet. Add 1 sliced onion and cook for 5 minutes, until softened. Stir in 1 crushed garlic clove and 5 oz mixed wild mushrooms. Cook for 3 minutes, then add 2 cooked chicken breasts, torn into shreds, 3 tablespoons crème fraîche or Greek yogurt, and 2 tablespoons chicken stock. Heat through, then add a handful of chopped dill and a good squeeze of lemon juice. Serve with garlic bread.

2 **Chicken, Mushroom, and Dill Strudels** Mix together 1 crushed garlic clove and 2 tablespoons olive oil. Toss with 2½ cups quartered mushrooms, place on a baking sheet, and cook in a preheated oven, at 400°F, for 3–5 minutes. Meanwhile, brush 4 tablespoons melted butter over 4 phyllo pastry sheets. Arrange ½ cooked chicken breast, torn into shreds, at one short end of each piece of pastry. Spoon over 1 tablespoon crème fraîche or sour cream, a little grated lemon rind, and some chopped dill. Sprinkle the cooked mushrooms on top, then fold over the long sides and roll up the pastry. Place the packages on the baking sheet and brush with more butter. Cook in the oven for 10–15 minutes, until golden and crisp.

1⦿ Melted Cheesy Chicken Tortilla Wedges

Serves 4

8 corn or wheat tortillas
2 cooked chicken breasts,
   torn into shreds
2 roasted red peppers, torn
   into strips
1 red chile, finely chopped
4 oz chorizo, thinly sliced
8 oz mozzarella cheese,
   thinly sliced
½ cup shredded sharp cheddar
   cheese
handful of chopped fresh cilantro
salt and black pepper
store-bought guacamole,
   to serve

- Lay 4 tortillas on 2 large baking sheets and sprinkle with the chicken, roasted red peppers, and chile. Divide the chorizo and cheese among the tortillas and sprinkle with the cilantro.

- Season to taste, place another tortilla on top of each to make a sandwich, then gently press down with your hand.

- Place in a preheated oven, at 375°F, and cook for 7 minutes, until lightly crisp and the cheese has melted. Cut into wedges, then serve with guacamole.

 Chicken Tortilla Packages Mix
2 cups cooked rice with ½ cup rinsed and drained canned black beans. Divide the rice mixture among 4 large tortillas. Sprinkle with 2 shredded, cooked chicken breasts, 2 chopped tomatoes, 1 tablespoon chopped shallot, the grated rind and juice of ½ lime, and some fresh cilantro. Sprinkle with ½ cup shredded cheddar cheese and top each with 1 tablespoon sour cream. Fold over the sides, then roll up the tortillas to form packages. Cook in a dry nonstick skillet for 3–5 minutes on each side until golden and crisp.

 Chicken Tortilla Rolls with Tomato Sauce Mix 2 cups tomato sauce with 1 tablespoon sweet chili sauce, 1 teaspoon ground cumin, and a pinch of ground cinnamon. Stir ½ cup of the mixture with 4 cooked chicken breasts, torn into shreds, and 2 roasted red peppers, cut into strips. Divide the chicken mixture among 8 tortillas, then roll up and place them, seam side down, in a shallow ovenproof dish. Pour the remaining tomato sauce over the top and sprinkle with ½ cup shredded cheddar cheese and 4 oz sliced mozzarella cheese.

Place in a preheated oven, at 400°F, for 20–25 minutes, until bubbling and heated through.

 # Steamed Soy Chicken with Mixed Mushrooms

Serves 4

4 small skinless chicken breasts
8 oz mixed mushrooms
⅓ cup soy sauce
finely grated rind and juice of
⅓ lime
1 chile, sliced
1 garlic clove, chopped
1 teaspoon finely grated fresh
ginger root
handful of chopped fresh cilantro,
to garnish
boiled jasmine rice (optional),
to serve

- Set a large steamer over a saucepan of gently simmering water. Place the chicken and mushrooms in a shallow, heatproof dish that will fit inside the steamer. Mix together the remaining ingredients and spoon the mixture over the chicken.

- Place the dish in the steamer, cover, and cook for 15 minutes, until the chicken is just cooked through. Sprinkle with cilantro and serve with jasmine rice, if desired.

 Soy-Fried Noodles with Chicken and Oyster Mushrooms Heat a wok until smoking hot. Add 2 tablespoons vegetable oil and 10 oz thinly sliced chicken breast. Stir-fry for 5 minutes, then add 1 crushed garlic clove, 1 teaspoon finely grated fresh ginger root, and 8 oz oyster mushrooms. Cook for another 2 minutes. Stir in 4 oz egg noodles, cooked, 4 cups baby spinach leaves, and ¼ cup soy sauce mixed with 1 tablespoon sweet chili sauce. Heat through until piping hot and serve immediately.

Roasted Soy Chicken with Shiitake Mushrooms Mix ¼ cup soy sauce with the finely grated rind of 1 lemon, a squeeze of lemon juice, 1 crushed garlic clove, and 1 finely chopped red chile. Marinate 4 skinless chicken breasts in the mixture for 5–10 minutes. Remove from the marinade and place in a shallow roasting pan. Dot with 2 tablespoons butter, cut into small cubes, then place in a preheated oven, at 400°F, for 15 minutes. Arrange 8 oz whole shiitake mushrooms around the chicken and pour the marinade over the top. Return to the oven for another 5 minutes, until the chicken and mushrooms are cooked through. Serve with plain noodles or rice, if desired.

 Indian-Style Chicken and Peppers

Serves 4

2 tablespoons vegetable oil

12 oz skinless chicken breasts, diced

1 onion, sliced

2 garlic cloves, chopped

1 tablespoon finely grated fresh ginger root

1 tablespoon ground coriander

1 teaspoon ground fenugreek

1 teaspoon garam masala

1 red bell pepper, cored, seeded, and sliced

1 green bell pepper, cored, seeded, and sliced

5 tomatoes, chopped

¼ cup heavy cream

2 tablespoons lemon juice

handful of chopped fresh cilantro, to garnish

Indian-style bread, to serve

- Heat the oil in a wok or large skillet. Add the chicken and cook for 5 minutes, until golden all over, then remove from the wok and set aside. Add the onion and cook for 5 minutes, until softened. Stir in the garlic and ginger and cook for 1 minute, then add the spices and stir around the wok.

- Add the bell peppers and stir until well coated. Stir in the tomatoes and chicken and cook for another 5–7 minutes, until the chicken is cooked through. Add the cream and lemon juice and season to taste. Sprinkle with the cilantro and serve with some warm Indian-style bread.

10 Chicken Pasta with Chile Pepper Pesto

Place 2 roasted red peppers in a food processor with ¼ cup toasted slivered almonds, 2 tablespoons mascarpone cheese, 1 teaspoon balsamic vinegar, a pinch of dried red pepper flakes, and a handful of chopped basil. Blend to form a paste. Cook 1 lb fresh penne according to the package directions, then drain. Stir in the pesto and 2 cooked chicken breasts, torn into strips. Sprinkle with grated Parmesan cheese.

30 Spicy Chicken and Pepper Casserole

Peel and thinly slice 1 lb new potatoes. Toss with 4 boneless, skinless chicken thighs, cut into chunks, 1 thickly sliced onion, 2 cored, seeded, and quartered red bell peppers, 3 tablespoons vegetable oil, and 2 teaspoons garam masala. Spread out on a large baking sheet and season to taste. Place in a preheated oven, at 425°F, and cook for 15 minutes. Give the baking sheet a good shake, add 8 cherry tomatoes and sprinkle with 1 teaspoon smoked paprika and the finely grated rind of 1 lemon. Return to the oven for another 10 minutes or until the chicken and potatoes are cooked through. Drizzle with some plain yogurt and sprinkle with chopped fresh cilantro to serve.

 Baked Chicken, Potatoes, and Asparagus with Gremolata

Serves 4

1 lb new potatoes, thinly sliced
3 tablespoons olive oil
4 chicken breasts
5 oz asparagus, trimmed
1 garlic clove, finely chopped

For the gremolata

finely grated rind of 1 lemon
large handful of chopped parsley
salt and black pepper

- Toss the potatoes with 2 tablespoons of the oil and place in a large, shallow roasting pan. Place in a preheated oven, at 400°F, for 5 minutes, then arrange the chicken breasts on top and drizzle with a little more oil. Season well and return to the oven for another 10 minutes.

- Arrange the asparagus spears in the pan, pour any remaining oil over them, and return to the oven for another 5 minutes, until golden and cooked through.

- To make the gremolata, mix together the garlic, lemon rind, and parsley. Sprinkle it over the chicken and vegetables before serving.

10 Spaghetti with Chicken and Asparagus in Creamy Gremolata Sauce Cook 12 oz quick-cook spaghetti in a large saucepan of lightly salted boiling water according to the package directions. Add 5 oz asparagus tips 3 minutes before the end of cooking, then add ½ cup frozen peas 1 minute before the end. Drain and return the pasta and vegetables to the pan. Add 2 cooked chicken breasts, cut into bite-size pieces, ⅓ cup crème fraîche or heavy cream, 1 crushed garlic clove, the finely grated rind of 1 lemon, a squeeze of lemon juice, and plenty of chopped parsley. Season to taste, heat through, and serve.

30 Chicken, Asparagus, and Gremolata Frittata Heat 2 tablespoons olive oil in a large, nonstick skillet. Add 4 oz asparagus tips and 1 crushed garlic clove and cook for 5 minutes, until tender. Mix 1 cooked chicken breast, cut into bite-size pieces, with 6 beaten eggs, the finely grated rind of 1 lemon, and a handful of chopped parsley. Season to taste and pour into the skillet, mix gently together, then cook over low heat for 15 minutes or until the egg is cooked through.

10 Linguine with Creamy Chicken Carbonara

Serves 4

1 lb fresh linguine pasta

2 cooked chicken breasts, torn into strips

1 egg, lightly beaten

¼ cup crème fraîche or heavy cream

finely grated rind of ½ lemon, plus 1 tablespoon juice

¼ cup grated Parmesan cheese

salt and black pepper

handful of chopped chives, to garnish

- Cook the linguine in a large saucepan of lightly salted boiling water according to the package directions. Drain, reserving a little of the cooking water, and return the pasta to the pan.

- Add the chicken to the pan with the egg, crème fraîche or heavy cream, lemon rind and juice, and half the Parmesan.

- Season to taste and stir together, adding a little of the cooking water to loosen, if necessary. Divide among bowls and sprinkle with the remaining Parmesan and the chives. Serve immediately.

 20 Penne with Creamy Pan-Fried Chicken Heat 1 tablespoon olive oil in a large, heavy saucepan. Add 2 oz pancetta or chopped bacon and cook until golden. Remove from the pan and set aside. Add 4 chicken breasts to the pan and cook for 5 minutes on each side. Return the pancetta to the pan along with ¼ cup hot chicken stock and ¼ cup heavy cream. Stir in 10 oz fresh penne pasta and simmer for 3 minutes, until the pasta is "al dente" and the chicken is cooked through. Stir in ⅓ cup frozen peas and 2 tablespoons lemon juice and heat through. Season to taste and serve sprinkled with chopped chives.

30 Pasta Gratin with Creamy Chicken and Leeks Heat 1 tablespoon olive oil in a flameproof skillet. Add 1 thinly sliced leek for and cook for 3 minutes to soften. Add 10 oz diced chicken breast and cook for another 2 minutes. Stir in 12 oz dried penne pasta and 3 cups hot chicken stock, bring to a boil, then reduce the heat and simmer for 10 minutes. Add 1 cup heavy cream and continue to cook for a few minutes, until the pasta is "al dente" and the chicken is cooked through. Season to taste. Mix ½ cup dried bread crumbs with ¼ cup grated Parmesan cheese and the finely grated rind of 1 lemon. Sprinkle with the pasta mixture and cook under a preheated hot broiler for 5 minutes, until bubbling and crisp.

20 Seared Duck and Figs with Watercress Salad

Serves 4

4 duck breasts
4 figs, halved
½ teaspoon ground cinnamon
1 tablespoon balsamic vinegar
1 teaspoon honey
finely grated rind and juice of
 ½ orange
2 bunches watercress
1 head endive, leaves separated
salt and black pepper

- Use a sharp knife to score a crisscross pattern on the skin of the duck and season to taste. Heat a large skillet until hot, add the duck, skin side down, and cook for 7 minutes. Pour away the excess oil and turn the duck over. Arrange the figs in the skillet and cook for another 5–7 minutes, until the duck is cooked through and the figs softened.

- Remove the duck from the skillet and cut into thick slices. Pour off any excess fat, then add the cinnamon, vinegar, honey, and orange rind and juice to the skillet and swirl around.

- Divide the watercress and endive among plates, place the figs and sliced duck on top, then spoon the warm dressing over the top and serve immediately.

Smoked Duck, Orange, and Fig Salad

Cut 4 figs in half, drizzle with a little olive oil and 1 teaspoon balsamic vinegar, then cook under a preheated hot broiler for 2 minutes on each side until lightly browned. Toss 3 bunches of watercress with 1 tablespoon sherry vinegar and 3 tablespoons olive oil and divide among serving plates. Peel 1 orange and cut into segments, then arrange on the plates with the broiled figs and 4 oz sliced smoked duck breast.

Duck with Spicy Fig Couscous

Use a sharp knife to score a crisscross pattern on the skin of 4 duck breasts and season to taste. Heat a large skillet until hot, add the duck, skin side down, and cook for 7 minutes. Pour away the excess oil and turn the duck over. Cook for another 5 minutes, adding 1 crushed garlic clove to the skillet for the last minute of cooking. Remove the skillet from the heat and remove the duck from the skillet. Add 1¼ cups couscous, 1½ cups hot chicken stock, and 4 chopped, dried figs to the skillet, cover tightly, and let sit for 7 minutes or until the couscous has softened. Add the finely grated rind and juice of ½ orange, then fork through 1 finely chopped red chile and a large handful of chopped mint. Serve the couscous with the duck, cut into thick slices.

3⬤ Herb-Roasted Turkey Breast with Pancetta and Beans

Serves 4

handful of chopped rosemary
handful of chopped parsley
2 tablespoons butter, softened
1¾ lb turkey breast
6 garlic cloves
¼ cup dry white wine
¼ cup hot chicken stock
4 prosciutto slices
2 (15 oz) cans lima beans, rinsed
  and drained
handful of plum or cherry
  tomatoes, coarsely chopped
¼ cup heavy cream
salt and black pepper

- Mix together the rosemary, three-quarters of the parsley, and the butter and smear over the turkey. Season to taste.

- Place in a roasting pan with the garlic cloves, pour the wine and stock into the pan, and arrange the prosciutto on top of the turkey. Place in a preheated oven, at 425°F, for 25 minutes.

- Put the beans, tomatoes, and cream into the roasting pan, adding a little water, if necessary. Season to taste, then return to the oven for another 3–5 minutes or until the turkey is cooked through and the beans are warm.

- Cut the turkey into slices and arrange on plates with the crispy prosciutto and the beans, sprinkled with the remaining parsley.

 Spaghetti with Turkey, Ham, and Beans Cook 1 lb fresh spaghetti in a large saucepan of lightly salted boiling water according to the package directions. Add 1 cup rinsed and drained, canned cannellini beans for the last minute of cooking. Drain and then return to the pan. Add 4 slices of cooked turkey, cut into strips, 2 slices of ham, cut into strips, and a handful of chopped plum or cherry tomatoes. Stir in ¼ cup crème fraîche or heavy cream and 2 cups arugula, then grate over plenty of Parmesan cheese to serve.

 Turkey, Bacon, and Bean Stew Mix 12 oz ground turkey with 2 finely chopped scallions, 1 finely chopped bacon slice, and 1 egg yolk, and season well. Roll the mixture into small balls. Heat 1 tablespoon oil in a deep skillet. Cook the balls for 5 minutes, until golden all over. Stir in 1 crushed garlic clove, then add ¾ cup canned diced tomatoes and simmer for 5–10 minutes, until the turkey balls are cooked through. Stir in 1 (15 oz) can lima beans, rinsed and drained, and heat through. Season to taste and sprinkle with parsley to serve.

QuickCook
Fish

Recipes listed by cooking time

10

Rice with Salmon and Lemon Dressing

Serves 4

2 cups jasmine rice

4 cups water

4 salmon fillets

1 inch piece of fresh ginger root,
  cut into matchsticks

1 red chile, sliced

4 lemon slices

½ cup frozen shelled
  edamame beans

1 tablespoon lemon juice

¼ cup soy sauce

1 tablespoon mirin
  (Japanese rice wine)

salt

1 scallion, sliced,
  to garnish

- Put the rice and measured water in a large, heavy casserole dish. Add a little salt and bring to a boil, then reduce the heat and simmer, uncovered, for 7 minutes, until most of the water has boiled away.

- Place the salmon on top, sprinkle with the ginger and chile, and arrange a lemon slice on each piece of fish. Cover and cook for another 7 minutes, until the fish is just cooked through.

- Sprinkle with the edamame beans and let steam for 1 minute, until heated through. Mix together the lemon juice, soy sauce, and mirin and pour over the fish, then serve sprinkled with the scallion.

 Soba Noodles with Salmon and Lime Dressing Cook 8 oz soba noodles according to the package directions. Drain, cool under cold running water, if necessary, and drain again. Mix ¼ cup soy sauce with 1 tablespoon mirin (Japanese rice wine) and a squeeze of lime juice, then toss with the noodles. Cut ¼ cucumber into thin slices and add to the noodles with 2 flaked smoked salmon fillets and 2 sliced scallions. Sprinkle with sesame seeds to serve.

Rice Noodles with Salmon and Lemon Teriyaki Dressing In a small bowl, mix 3 tablespoons soy sauce with 2 tablespoons mirin (Japanese rice wine) and 2 teaspoons finely grated fresh ginger root. Drizzle the soy sauce mixture over 4 salmon fillets and let marinate for about 15 minutes. Heat 1 tablespoon olive oil in a skillet. Shake the excess marinade from the salmon and cook for 5–7 minutes, until starting to flake, then remove from the skillet and set aside. Heat another tablespoon oil and cook 1 sliced shallot for 3 minutes, then stir in 1 crushed garlic clove and 1½ cups snow peas. Cook for 2 minutes, until softened. Add 4 oz rice noodles, cooked, the salmon marinade, 1 teaspoon sugar, and a splash of water. Stir-fry for 1 minute, then return the salmon to the skillet with ¼ cup lemon juice and heat through.

ONE-FISH-JAA

30 Shrimp and Pea Risotto

Serves 4

2 tablespoons olive oil
1 onion, finely chopped
1½ cups risotto rice
½ cup dry white wine
4 cups hot fish or chicken stock
8 oz cooked peeled shrimp
1 cup frozen peas
finely grated rind of 1 lemon
2 tablespoons butter
2 tablespoons lemon juice
salt and black pepper
handful of chopped mint leaves,
   to garnish

- Heat the oil in a large, heavy saucepan. Add the onion and cook for 5 minutes, until softened. Stir in the risotto rice, followed by the wine, and simmer until reduced by half.

- Gradually add the stock, a ladleful at a time, stirring continuously and allowing each ladleful to be absorbed before adding the next. Continue to cook for about 15 minutes, or until the rice is tender.

- Stir in the shrimp, peas, lemon rind, and butter and season to taste. Cover and let rest for a few minutes, then add the lemon juice and serve sprinkled with the mint.

---

1 **Stir-Fried Rice with Shrimp and Peas**

Heat 1 tablespoon vegetable oil in a wok or large skillet. Add 1 crushed garlic clove and 1 teaspoon finely grated fresh ginger root and cook for 1 minute, then crack 1 egg into the wok and stir around to scramble. Add 2 cups cooked rice, 8 oz cooked, peeled shrimp, ⅔ cup frozen peas, and 1–2 tablespoons soy sauce. Heat through and serve immediately.

2 **Shrimp, Pea, and Rice Soup**

Heat 1 tablespoon olive oil in a large, heavy saucepan. Add 2 finely chopped shallots and 1 crushed garlic clove and cook for 3 minutes, until softened. Add 8 cups hot chicken stock and ½ cup long grain rice and simmer for 15 minutes. Stir in 8 oz cooked, peeled shrimp and ⅓ cup frozen fava beans. Cook for 1 minute, then add ⅓ cup frozen peas, the finely grated rind of 1 lemon, ½ finely chopped red chile, and a handful of chopped mint and heat through. Serve in warm bowls with 1 tablespoon crème fraîche or Greek yogurt in each.

30 Spanish Monkfish and Clam Stew

Serves 4

3 tablespoons olive oil

1 onion, chopped

1 garlic clove, sliced

1 red bell pepper, cored, seeded, and sliced

pinch of dried red pepper flakes

1 rosemary sprig

1 bay leaf

½ cup dry white wine

pinch of saffron threads

1 (14½ oz) can diced tomatoes

¾ cup blanched almonds, toasted and ground

1¼ lb monkfish, cut into bite-size pieces

1 lb clams, rinsed and drained

salt and black pepper

- Heat the oil in a wide saucepan or flameproof casserole dish. Add the onion and cook for 5 minutes, until softened. Add the garlic and red bell pepper and cook for another 2 minutes, then stir in the red pepper flakes and herbs and pour in the wine.

- Bring to a boil, then reduce the heat and simmer for 2 minutes. Add the saffron and tomatoes and simmer for another 10 minutes, then stir in the almonds.

- Add the monkfish to the stew and cook for 3 minutes. Add the clams, cover the pan with a tightly fitting lid, and continue to cook for about 5 minutes, until the clams have opened, discarding any that have not. Remove the herbs and season the stew to taste.

---

10 Monkfish with Clam and Tomato Sauce

Heat 2 tablespoons olive oil in a large skillet. Add 1 lb monkfish medallions and cook for 3 minutes on each side. Stir in 1 chopped garlic clove and cook for 30 seconds, then add 1¼ cups canned baby clams, drained, and 6 halved cherry tomatoes. Cook for 2 minutes, season well, then sprinkle with ¼ cup toasted slivered almonds and a handful of chopped parsley.

20 Monkfish, Clam, and Tomato

Packages Cut 4 large squares of aluminum foil. Divide 1 lb monkfish, cut into medallions, among the packages and top with 6 halved cherry tomatoes. Add 1 rosemary sprig and 3 clams, rinsed and drained, to each. Season with salt and black pepper, fold the foil over, and roll up the edges to create airtight packages, leaving just a little gap. Mix ¼ cup dry white wine with a pinch of saffron threads, pour a little into each package, and then fully seal, leaving enough space in the packages for air to circulate. Place on a baking sheet and cook in a preheated oven, at 425°F, for 15 minutes, until the packages have puffed up and the clams have opened. Discard any clams that have not opened. Serve with crusty bread.

30 Crispy Fish Pie

Serves 4

butter, for greasing
1⅓ cups frozen spinach (about two-thirds of a 10 oz package)
12 oz skinless salmon fillet, cubed
8 oz skinless smoked haddock fillet, cubed
4 eggs
½ cup crème fraîche or heavy cream
2 tablespoons boiling water
½ cup dried bread crumbs
salt and black pepper

- Lightly grease an ovenproof dish. Place the spinach in a strainer and pour boiling water over it until defrosted. Lay the spinach on a sheet of paper towels and squeeze to get rid of excess water.

- Arrange the spinach in the ovenproof dish and place the fish on top. Make 4 small holes between the fish pieces and crack an egg into each one.

- Mix the crème fraîche or heavy cream with the measured water and season to taste. Pour it over the fish, then sprinkle with the bread crumbs. Place in a preheated oven, at 400°F, for 25 minutes or until golden and bubbling and the fish is cooked through.

 Crispy Fish Nuggets

Cut 12 oz chunky skinless salmon fillet into small bite-size pieces and toss with 3 tablespoons olive oil. Place 1 cup dried white bread crumbs, the finely grated rind of 1 lemon, a handful of chopped parsley, and a pinch of salt in a plastic food bag. Add the salmon and shake until well coated, then arrange the pieces on a lightly greased baking sheet. Drizzle with another tablespoon oil, then cook under a preheated hot broiler for 5 minutes. Turn over and cook for another 2–3 minutes, until golden and cooked through. Serve with a tomato salad.

 Fish Gratins with Crispy Topping

Divide 8 oz skinless, smoked haddock fillet, cut into small pieces, between 4 ramekins. Stir together ⅓ cup crème fraîche or heavy cream, a handful of chopped chives, and 2 tablespoons water, then stir into the fish. Place in a preheated oven, at 350°F, for 5–7 minutes. Crack an egg on top of each ramekin, top with a sprinkling of dried bread crumbs and a drizzle of melted butter, then return to the oven for another 10–12 minutes, until the eggs are set. Serve with crusty bread.

20 Steamed Lemon Dill Salmon and Potatoes

Serves 2

12 oz new potatoes, sliced
2 salmon fillets
¾ cup trimmed green beans
¼ cup crème fraîche or
   Greek yogurt
finely grated rind and juice of
   ½ lemon
handful of chopped dill
1 tablespoon capers, rinsed
   and drained
salt and black pepper

- Set a large steamer over a saucepan of gently simmering water. Place the potatoes in a shallow, heatproof dish that will fit inside the steamer and season well. Cover and cook for 10 minutes.

- Place the salmon on top of the potatoes and sprinkle the beans around them. Cook for another 7–10 minutes or until the fish and vegetables are cooked through.

- Meanwhile, mix together the crème fraîche, lemon rind and juice, dill, and capers and season to taste. Serve with the salmon and vegetables.

Salmon with Creamy Lemon Dill Beans Heat 1 tablespoon olive oil in a skillet. Add 2 salmon fillets, skin side down, and cook for 5 minutes. Turn over and cook for another 1 minute. Add 1 cup canned cannellini beans, rinsed and drained, to the skillet with ¼ cup hot chicken stock and 3 tablespoons crème fraîche or heavy cream. Season to taste, heat through, then stir in the finely grated rind of 1 lemon and a handful of chopped dill. Serve with crusty bread.

Roasted Salmon, Potatoes, and Asparagus with Lemon Dill Dressing Toss 2 tablespoons olive oil with 3 potatoes, cut into cubes. Place in a shallow roasting pan and cook in a preheated oven, at 400°F, for 15 minutes, stirring halfway through cooking. Arrange 2 salmon fillets and 4–6 asparagus spears in the pan, season to taste, and return to the oven for another 12–15 minutes, until cooked through. Mix 2 tablespoons olive oil with the finely grated rind and juice of ½ lemon and a handful of chopped dill, season to taste, and drizzle with the salmon and vegetables before serving.

10 Chile Shrimp Noodles

Serves 4

1/3 cup ketchup

2 tablespoons light soy sauce

2 teaspoons sugar

2 teaspoons cornstarch

2/3 cup water

2 tablespoons vegetable oil

1 red bell pepper, seeded
  and sliced

2 garlic cloves, crushed

2 teaspoons finely grated fresh
  ginger root

1–2 red chiles, finely chopped

8 oz cooked, peeled shrimp

4 oz egg noodles, cooked

1 lime

2 scallions, sliced

- Stir together the ketchup, soy sauce, sugar, cornstarch, and measured water until smooth, then set aside. Heat a large wok or skillet. Add the oil and swirl around the wok, then add the red bell pepper and cook for 2 minutes.

- Stir in the garlic, ginger, and chile and stir-fry for 1 minute, then add the shrimp and the ketchup mixture and cook for 3 minutes, until thickened.

- Add the noodles to the wok and cook until heated through and coated with the sauce. Squeeze the lime juice over the noodles, sprinkle with the scallions, and serve immediately.

20 Chile Shrimp and Lime Couscous

Cook 1 finely chopped onion in 2 tablespoons oil for 5 minutes, then stir in 1 crushed garlic clove, 1 teaspoon chopped fresh ginger root, 1 chopped red chile, and 1/2 teaspoon ground cumin. Cook for 1 minute, then stir in 8 oz peeled shrimp and cook for 2 minutes. Remove from the heat, add 1 1/2 cups couscous and 1 1/2 cups hot fish stock, cover, and let rest for 5 minutes. Add some chopped cilantro, 1 sliced scallion, and the finely grated rind and juice of 1 lime, then fork through the couscous.

30 Chile Shrimp Bisque

Remove the shells from 1 lb large shrimp and chop the shells into small pieces. Heat 2 tablespoons vegetable oil in a large saucepan and cook the shells with 1 chopped onion until the onion is soft. Add 1 teaspoon tomato paste, 1–2 chopped red chiles, 2 chopped garlic cloves, a 1 inch piece of fresh ginger root, and 1 lemon grass stalk and cook for 1 minute, then add 3 chopped tomatoes, 6 cups hot fish or chicken stock, and 1/3 cup rice. Bring to a boil, then reduce the heat and simmer for 15–20 minutes, until the rice is cooked. Remove the lemon grass and ginger, then pour the soup into a blender and process until smooth. Pass through a strainer back into the pan. Add the shrimp, 1/2 cup coconut milk, and 1 tablespoon Thai fish sauce and cook for 3 minutes, until the shrimp are cooked through. Sprinkle with chopped fresh cilantro to serve.

20 Spicy Fish and Potato Soup

Serves 4

1 tablespoon olive oil

2 garlic cloves, chopped

½ teaspoon ground cumin

½ teaspoon dried red pepper flakes

5 cups hot fish or chicken stock

1 lb small new potatoes, halved if large

3 tomatoes, chopped

12 oz skinless firm white fish fillets, cut into pieces

1 tablespoon lemon juice

salt and black pepper

To garnish

handful of chopped mint

handful of chopped cilantro

- Heat the oil in a large, heavy saucepan. Add the garlic and cook for 30 seconds, then stir in the spices and stock and season to taste. Add the potatoes and bring to a boil, then reduce the heat and simmer for 12 minutes.

- Add the tomatoes and fish and cook for about 5 minutes, until cooked through. Add the lemon juice, taste, and adjust the seasoning, if necessary. Ladle the soup into bowls and serve sprinkled with the herbs.

---

10 Spicy Broiled Fish with Chickpea Salad

Mix 1 teaspoon ground cumin with a pinch of dried red pepper flakes, a pinch of salt, and 1 tablespoon olive oil. Spread over 4 thin white fish fillets arranged on a baking sheet. Cook under a preheated hot broiler for 7–9 minutes or until cooked through. Toss together 1 (15 oz) can chickpeas, rinsed and drained, ½ cup chopped sun-dried tomatoes in oil, the finely grated rind of 1 lemon, and a squeeze of lemon juice. Season to taste and serve with the fish and its juices, sprinkled with chopped cilantro.

30 Baked Fish and Potatoes with Spicy Herb Dressing

Toss 1½ lb new potatoes, halved if large, with 2 tablespoons olive oil and ½ teaspoon ground cumin. Place in a roasting pan and cook in a preheated oven, at 425°F, for 15 minutes. Add 4 white fish fillets and 6 cherry tomatoes, season to taste, then return to the oven for another 10–15 minutes, until the fish is cooked through. Meanwhile, place a large bunch of fresh cilantro in a food processor with 1 chopped red chile, 1 teaspoon ground cumin, 3 ground cardamom pods, and ⅓ cup olive oil and blend together to make a dressing. Drizzle it over the vegetables and fish before serving.

30 Baked Bacon-Wrapped Trout with Horseradish Sauce

Serves 4

1½ lb potatoes, thinly sliced

3 tablespoons olive oil

4 small whole trout,
  gutted and scaled

1 lemon, sliced

4 thyme sprigs, plus extra
  to serve

4 thin bacon slices

1 tablespoon horseradish sauce

1 cup crème fraîche or
  heavy cream

salt and black pepper

- Toss the potatoes with the oil, season to taste, and place in a shallow roasting pan. Place in a preheated oven, at 425°F for 15 minutes, until starting to turn golden.

- Meanwhile, stuff the cavity of each trout with 2 lemon slices and a thyme sprig. Wrap 1 bacon slice around each one, then arrange in the roasting pan. Return to the oven for another 12–15 minutes, until the fish and potatoes are cooked through.

- Meanwhile, mix the horseradish sauce with the crème fraiche or heavy cream. Serve with the potatoes and fish, sprinkled with some thyme.

---

10 Smoked Trout and Bacon Salad with Horseradish Dressing Cook 4 bacon slices under a preheated hot broiler for about 7 minutes, until crisp, then break into pieces. Mix 2 teaspoons horseradish sauce with ½ cup heavy cream and add lemon juice to taste. Place 1 (7 oz) package mixed salad greens in a bowl with ½ sliced cucumber. Arrange 2 flaked smoked trout fillets on top, sprinkle with the bacon, then drizzle with the dressing.

20 Bacon-Wrapped Trout with Crispy Crumbs and Horseradish Cream Wrap 1 bacon slice and a rosemary sprig around each of 4 small gutted and scaled trout. Arrange in a shallow roasting pan with 1 lemon, cut into wedges. Drizzle with 1 tablespoon olive oil and cook in a preheated oven, at 400°F, for 7 minutes. Tear 4 thick slices of white bread into chunks and sprinkle around the fish. Return to the oven for another 7 minutes or until the fish is cooked through. Sprinkle with ¼ cup toasted slivered almonds. Whip ½ cup heavy cream until soft peaks form, then stir in 1 tablespoon horseradish sauce and a little finely grated lemon rind. Serve the fish with the crispy crumbs, a handful of arugula leaves, and the horseradish cream.

 # Clam, Kale, and Lima Bean Stew

Serves 4

1 tablespoon olive oil
2 oz chorizo, chopped
1 onion, finely chopped
2 garlic cloves, chopped
1 teaspoon tomato paste
¼ cup dry white wine
1 cup hot chicken stock
1 cup chopped kale
1 lb clams, rinsed and drained
1 cup canned lima beans,
   rinsed and drained
salt and black pepper

- Heat the oil in a large saucepan or flameproof casserole dish. Add the chorizo and cook for 1 minute, until starting to release its oil. Add the onion and cook for another 5 minutes, until softened, then stir in the garlic and tomato paste and cook for 1 minute.

- Pour in the wine and let it simmer until reduced by half. Add the stock and kale and cook for 5 minutes.

- Add the clams, cover, and cook for 3 minutes, then stir in the beans. Cover and cook for another 3 minutes, until the clams have opened, discarding any that have not. Season to taste and serve.

10 Stir-Fried Clams and Kale in Black Bean Sauce

Heat 2 tablespoons oil in a wok. Add 2 sliced garlic cloves and cook for a few seconds, then add 2 cups chopped kale and stir-fry for 1–2 minutes. Add ½ finely chopped chile and 2 teaspoons finely grated fresh ginger root and stir in, then add 1 lb clams, rinsed and drained, and ⅓ cup black bean sauce. Add a splash of water, cover, and cook for 5 minutes, until the clams have opened, discarding any that have not. Sprinkle with 1 sliced scallion before serving with plain rice, if desired.

30 Clam, Lemon, and Spinach Risotto

Heat 2 tablespoons olive oil in a large, heavy saucepan. Add 1 finely chopped onion and cook for 5 minutes, until softened, then add 2 crushed garlic cloves and cook for another 30 seconds. Stir in 1½ cups risotto rice, followed by ½ cup dry white wine, and let simmer until boiled away. Gradually add 4 cups hot chicken stock, a ladleful at a time, stirring continuously and allowing each ladleful to be absorbed before adding the next. After 10 minutes, add 12 oz clams, rinsed and drained, and cook for another 5 minutes, until the rice is tender and the clams have opened, discarding any that have not. Add the finely grated rind of ½ lemon, 3 cups baby spinach leaves, and ½ cup mascarpone cheese, then heat through and serve.

 # Spicy Salmon with Couscous

Serves 4

1 tablespoon olive oil, plus extra
   for greasing
1 teaspoon ground cumin
½ teaspoon ground coriander
pinch of dried red pepper flakes
finely grated rind of 1 lemon
4 skinless salmon fillets
2 teaspoons honey
1½ cups couscous
1½ cups hot chicken
   or fish stock
2 scallions, sliced
¼ cup toasted, slivered almonds
handful of chopped fresh cilantro
salt and black pepper

- Lightly grease a small roasting pan. Mix together the oil, spices, and lemon rind and rub all over the salmon, season to taste, and arrange in the roasting pan.

- Place in a preheated oven, at 400°F, for 10 minutes, drizzle with the honey, and return to the oven for another 3 minutes, until golden and cooked through.

- Remove from the oven, sprinkle the couscous around the salmon, and pour in the stock. Cover tightly with aluminum foil and let rest for 5 minutes, until the couscous is tender.

- Transfer the salmon to plates. Stir the scallions, almonds, and cilantro into the couscous and serve with the salmon.

Hot-Smoked Salmon Couscous Tabbouleh

Put 1½ cups couscous into a bowl and pour 1½ cups hot chicken stock over it. Cover and let rest for 5 minutes, until the couscous is soft. Mix the finely grated rind and juice of ½ lemon with ½ teaspoon ground cumin and 3 tablespoons olive oil, season to taste, and stir through the couscous, fluffing it up. Add ¼ cucumber, finely chopped, 2 chopped tomatoes, 1 sliced scallion, a large handful of chopped parsley, and 8 oz smoked salmon, toss together, and serve.

Couscous-Crusted Salmon

Put ¾ cup couscous into a bowl and pour ¾ cup hot chicken stock over it. Cover and let rest for 5 minutes, until the couscous is tender. Add ¼ cup chopped, pitted ripe black olives, the finely grated rind of 1 orange, and a handful of chopped parsley, season to taste, and stir to fluff up. Brush 4 large, skinless salmon fillets with 2 tablespoons olive oil, then dip the fillets in the couscous until well coated. Place on a greased baking sheet and cook in a preheated oven, at 400°F, for 12–15 minutes, until the salmon is cooked through. Serve with green salad.

30 Smoked Haddock Kedgeree

Serves 4

1 tablespoon vegetable oil
2 tablespoons butter
1 onion, finely chopped
1 garlic clove, crushed
1 teaspoon finely grated
   fresh ginger root
1 teaspoon cumin seeds
½ teaspoon coriander seeds
1 teaspoon curry powder
½ teaspoon ground turmeric
1½ cups basmati rice or other
   long grain rice
2¾ cups hot chicken or fish stock
10 oz skinless, smoked
   haddock fillet
½ cup frozen peas
1 red chile, chopped
handful of chopped fresh cilantro
salt and black pepper
mango chutney, to serve

- Heat the oil and butter in a large saucepan. Add the onion and cook for 5 minutes, then stir in the garlic and ginger and cook for 1 minute. Add the cumin seeds and coriander seeds and cook for 30 seconds, then stir in the curry powder, turmeric, and rice and cook for another 1 minute.

- Pour in the stock and cook for 5 minutes. Place the fish fillet on top of the rice and cook for another 5 minutes. By this time, most of the stock should have boiled away. Add the peas, cover the pan tightly with a lid, turn down the heat as low as it will go, and cook for 5–7 minutes, until the rice is cooked through.

- Use a fork to gently break up the fish, stir the fish and peas into the rice, and season to taste with salt and black pepper. Sprinkle with the chile and cilantro and serve with mango chutney.

 Smoked Haddock in Creamy Curry Sauce Heat 1 tablespoon vegetable oil in a deep skillet. Add 1 finely chopped shallot and cook for 2 minutes, until softened. Stir in 1 teaspoon curry powder, then arrange 4 smoked haddock fillets in the skillet. Cook for 1 minute, then pour in a splash of white wine and ½ cup hot fish or chicken stock. Bring to a boil, then cover the skillet and simmer for 5 minutes, until the fish is cooked through. Stir in 2 tablespoons crème fraîche or heavy cream, then arrange the fish on plates and spoon the sauce on top. Serve with boiled rice, if desired.

 Smoked Haddock, Rice, and Spinach Soup Cook 1 chopped onion in 1 tablespoon oil for 5 minutes, then add ½ cup long grain rice, 6 cups hot chicken or fish stock, and a pinch of saffron threads. Simmer for 10 minutes, then add 10 oz skinless, smoked haddock fillet and cook for 3 minutes, until starting to break up. Add ½ cup light cream and 3½ cups baby spinach leaves and heat through until wilted.

ONE-FISH-RUO

Thai Hot-and-Sour Shrimp Soup

Serves 4

1 tablespoon tom yum or Thai red
  curry paste
6 cups hot chicken or fish stock
¾ inch piece of fresh ginger root
1 lemon grass stalk
2 kaffir lime leaves
1 teaspoon packed light
  brown sugar
1 tablespoon Thai fish sauce
13 oz oyster mushrooms, sliced
8 oz large shrimp
lime juice, to taste
handful of chopped fresh cilantro,
  to garnish

- Heat a large, heavy saucepan. Add the curry paste, then stir in the stock, ginger, lemon grass, lime leaves, sugar, and fish sauce. Bring to a boil, then reduce the heat and simmer for 5 minutes.

- Add the mushrooms and shrimp and season to taste. Cook for another 3–4 minutes, until the shrimp are just cooked through. Add lime juice to taste, remove the ginger, lemon grass, and lime leaves, if desired, and serve immediately, sprinkled with the cilantro.

 Thai Spicy Shrimp Soup with Sweet Potato Heat 1 tablespoon vegetable oil in a large, heavy saucepan. Add 1 tablespoon Thai red curry paste and cook for 1 minute, then add 6 cups hot chicken stock and bring to a boil. Add a ¾ inch piece of fresh ginger root, 1 kaffir lime leaf, and 1 lemon grass stalk and simmer for 5 minutes. Add 1 large sweet potato, peeled and cubed, and cook for 7–10 minutes, until tender. Add 8 oz cooked, large shrimp and heat through. Serve sprinkled with 1 chopped red chile and cilantro leaves.

Thai Hot-and-Sour Shrimp Jungle Curry Place 2 tablespoons chopped fresh ginger root, 1 crushed garlic clove, 1 chopped green chile, 1 chopped lemon grass stalk, 1 small shallot, and a handful of fresh cilantro in a small food processor and blend to a smooth paste. Peel 8 oz large shrimp. Heat 2 tablespoons vegetable oil in a large saucepan, add the shrimp shells, and cook for 5 minutes, crushing as you work, until golden. Add the paste and cook for 2 minutes, until fragrant. Add 2 tablespoons Thai fish sauce, 1 cup hot vegetable or chicken stock, and 2 kaffir lime leaves and simmer for 10 minutes. Strain the liquid, return to the pan, and add 1 chopped eggplant. Cook for 5 minutes to soften, then add the shrimp, 1½ cups snake beans or green beans and ¾ cup cooked bamboo shoots. Cook for 3–5 minutes, until the shrimp are cooked through. Sprinkle with chopped fresh cilantro to serve.

ONE-FISH-MAA

30 Baked Tuna with Ratatouille

Serves 4

1 onion, cut into wedges

1 eggplant, cut into chunks

1 red bell pepper, cored, seeded, and cut into chunks

1 zucchini, thickly sliced

4 tomatoes, quartered

⅓ cup olive oil

2 garlic cloves, crushed

1 tablespoon sherry vinegar

4 tuna steaks

salt and black pepper

handful of chopped basil, to garnish

- Toss the vegetables with 3 tablespoons of the oil, arrange in a shallow roasting dish, and season to taste. Place in a preheated oven, at 400°F, for 15 minutes, turning occasionally, until lightly browned.

- Mix the remaining oil with the garlic and vinegar and stir into the vegetables. Arrange the tuna steaks in the dish and season well. Return to the oven for another 12–15 minutes, until the tuna is cooked. Serve immediately, sprinkled with the basil.

10 Seared Tuna with Ratatouille Salad

Rub 1 tablespoon olive oil over 4 tuna steaks and season to taste. Cook in a preheated, hot ridged grill pan for 2–3 minutes on each side until golden on the outside but still pink in the middle. Set aside. Mix together 2 teaspoons balsamic vinegar, 3 tablespoons olive oil, and 1 crushed garlic clove. Season to taste. Toss with 1 (5 oz) package arugula, 1 roasted red pepper from a jar, 1 roasted eggplant from a jar, cut into strips, and 6–8 halved cherry tomatoes. Serve the salad with the tuna.

20 Roasted Tuna with Ratatouille

Topping Rub 1 tablespoon olive oil over 4 tuna steaks and place in a shallow roasting pan. Sprinkle 4 halved cherry tomatoes, 1 cored, seeded, and chopped red bell pepper, 1 sliced garlic clove, and 1 tablespoon capers, rinsed and drained, over the fish, season well, and drizzle with another tablespoon oil. Place in a preheated oven, at 400°F, for 12–15 minutes, until the vegetables are lightly browned and the tuna is cooked. Sprinkle with chopped basil before serving with crusty bread.

 # Baked Cod Packages with Beans and Chorizo

Serves 4

4 cod fillets
1 (15 oz) canned lima beans, rinsed and drained
6–8 cherry tomatoes, halved
4 thyme sprigs
4 thin chorizo slices
⅓ cup dry white wine
salt and black pepper

• Cut 4 large sheets of parchment paper and place a cod fillet on each. Divide the beans, tomatoes, and thyme among the packages and season well.

• Place a chorizo slice on top of each piece of fish and season with salt and black pepper, then fold the paper over and roll up the edges to create airtight packages, leaving just a little gap.

• Pour a little wine into each package and then fully seal, leaving enough space in the packages for air to circulate. Place on a baking sheet and cook in a preheated oven, at 425°F, for 15 minutes, until the fish is cooked through.

 ### Seared Cod with Bean and Tomato Salad

Rub 1 tablespoon olive oil over 4 cod fillets and season well. Place skin side down in a preheated ridged grill pan and cook for 5 minutes. Turn over and cook for another 3 minutes until golden and cooked through. Meanwhile, beat together 1 tablespoon balsamic vinegar and 3 tablespoons olive oil. Add 14–16 halved cherry tomatoes and 1 (15 oz) can lima beans, rinsed and drained. Season to taste and add 5 cups arugula and ½ chopped red chile. Serve the salad with the cod.

 ### Spicy Cod and Bean Stew

Heat 2 tablespoons olive oil in a flameproof casserole dish. Add 3 chopped bacon slices and cook for 2 minutes, until golden, then add 1 chopped onion and cook for 5 minutes, until softened. Stir in 2 crushed garlic cloves and 1 teaspoon smoked paprika. Pour in ⅓ cup dry white wine and cook for another 3 minutes. Add 2 chopped tomatoes and 2 thyme sprigs and simmer for 5 minutes. Season well, then add 1 cup rinsed and drained canned lima beans and heat through. Slide 4 cod fillets into the stew, cover tightly, and cook for 12–15 minutes, until the fish is cooked through. Sprinkle with chopped parsley before serving.

ONE-FISH-JYA

10 Sea Bass with Herb and Olive Couscous

Serves 4

¼ cup dry white wine
1½ cup couscous
1½ cup hot vegetable stock
4 sea bass fillets
2 tablespoons extra virgin olive oil
½ cup pitted ripe black olives
1 roasted red pepper from a jar,
   sliced
handful of chopped basil
handful of chopped parsley
salt and black pepper

- Pour the wine into a shallow, flameproof casserole dish and boil for 1 minute. Add the couscous and stock and stir well, then arrange the fish on top. Cover and let cook gently for 8 minutes, until the fish and couscous are cooked through.

- Transfer the fish to warm plates, stir the remaining ingredients into the couscous, season to taste, and serve with the fish.

20 Roasted Pepper and Sea Bass

Baked with Couscous Cut a red bell pepper into wedges and arrange in a shallow roasting pan with 4 sea bass fillets and 3 garlic cloves. Rub 2 tablespoons olive oil over the ingredients in the pan, season to taste, and place in a preheated oven, at 425°F, for 10 minutes. Add 1½ cups couscous and 1½ cups hot vegetable stock to the pan. Cover with aluminum foil and return to the oven for another 5 minutes. Let steam, covered, for a few more minutes, until cooked through. Stir in ¼ cup lemon juice, 1 sliced scallion, and a handful of chopped basil and serve immediately.

30 Spicy Sea Bass and Couscous Stew

Heat 2 tablespoons olive oil in a large, heavy saucepan. Add 1 chopped onion and cook for 5 minutes, until softened. Stir in 1 crushed garlic clove and cook for 30 seconds. Add 1 teaspoon ground cumin, 1 cinnamon stick, ¾ cup canned diced tomatoes, and 2 cups hot vegetable stock. Season to taste, add a pinch of saffron threads, and simmer for 10 minutes. Add 1 sliced red bell pepper and 1 cup couscous and cook for 3 minutes. Add 4 sea bass fillets, cut into bite-size pieces, and continue to cook for about 5 minutes, until cooked through. Sprinkle with parsley to serve.

Fish, Coconut, and Potato Curry

Serves 4

2 tablespoons vegetable oil
1 teaspoon mustard seeds
½ teaspoon fenugreek seeds
1 onion, sliced
2 garlic cloves, finely chopped
1 tablespoon finely grated fresh ginger root
1 green chile, chopped
1 teaspoon ground turmeric
1 teaspoon ground coriander
1 stalk of curry leaves
1 tablespoon tamarind paste
1¾ cups coconut milk
12 oz new potatoes, halved
8 cherry tomatoes, halved
12 oz skinless cod or haddock fillet, cut into chunks

- Heat the oil in a large saucepan. Add the mustard and fenugreek seeds and cook for 30 seconds, until they sizzle. Add the onion and cook for 3–4 minutes, until softened.

- Stir in the garlic, ginger, and chile, followed by the ground spices and curry leaves and cook for 1 minute. Add the tamarind and coconut milk, season to taste, and bring to a boil.

- Add the potatoes and cook for 7 minutes, then add the tomatoes and fish and simmer for another 7 minutes, until the fish and potatoes are cooked through.

 Fish and Coconut Tikka

Mix 3 tablespoons coconut cream with 1 tablespoon tikka curry paste. Stir in 12 oz skinless cod fillet, cut into thick chunks. Thread the fish onto metal skewers, alternating with whole cherry tomatoes. Drizzle with a little vegetable oil, and cook under a preheated hot broiler for 4 minutes on each side until cooked through. Serve wrapped in chapattis with some green salad and dried coconut.

 Baked Spicy Fish, Coconut, and Potatoes

Place 2 crushed garlic cloves, 2 teaspoons finely grated fresh ginger root, 1 chopped red chile, 1 teaspoon ground cumin, 1 teaspoon ground coriander, a pinch of turmeric, 1 tablespoon vegetable oil, and ¼ cup coconut milk in a food processor and blend until smooth. Season. Make 3 slashes across each side of a whole gutted and scaled 2½ lb sea bass. Rub the paste over the fish and place 2 lemon slices inside the cavity. Place in a lightly oiled roasting pan with 1 lb new potatoes, thinly sliced. Pour in ½ cup water, cover with aluminum foil, and place in a preheated oven, at 400°F, for 15 minutes. Remove the foil and arrange 5 large tomatoes, quartered, around the fish. Return to the oven for about 10 minutes, until the fish and potatoes are cooked through. Serve sprinkled with cilantro leaves and serve with a crisp green salad.

30 Baked Prosciutto-Wrapped Monkfish with Tapenade

Serves 4

1½ lb new potatoes

2 tablespoons olive oil

15 prosciutto slices

12 oz monkfish, boned and cut into 4 fillets

1 red bell pepper, cored, seeded, and cut into chunks

handful of chopped parsley

¼ cup tapenade (olive paste)

salt and black pepper

- Toss the potatoes with the oil, season to taste, and place in a large, shallow roasting pan. Place in a preheated oven, at 425°F, for 5 minutes.

- Meanwhile, lay the prosciutto slices on a large piece of wax paper so they are slightly overlapping. Season the monkfish fillets and place side by side on the prosciutto, with one thick end and one thin end at each side to make a uniform shape. Use the wax paper to help you lift the prosciutto up and over the fish so it is tightly wrapped.

- Give the potatoes a good shake, then add the monkfish and red bell pepper to the pan. Return to the oven for another 15–20 minutes, until the fish and potatoes are cooked through. Meanwhile, stir the parsley into the tapenade, then serve with the fish and vegetables.

 Prosciutto-Wrapped Monkfish Skewers Cut 12 oz monkfish tail into bite-size pieces and wrap half a slice of prosciutto around each one. Thread onto metal skewers, alternating with chunks of red bell pepper and leaving a little space at the end. Drizzle with 1 tablespoon olive oil and cook under a preheated hot broiler for 2 minutes. Thread ¼ baguette, cut into chunks, onto the ends of the skewers, drizzle with a little more oil, and cook for 5 minutes, turning occasionally, until the fish is cooked through. Serve with a green salad tossed with ½ cup pitted ripe black olives.

 Baked Prosciutto-Wrapped Monkfish Cutlets Cut 12 oz monkfish tail into ¾ inch slices. Wrap a slice of prosciutto around each piece of fish and arrange close together in a roasting pan, tucking slices of red bell pepper between them. Chop 3 tomatoes and mix with ½ cup coarsely chopped ripe black olives, 1 crushed garlic clove, the finely grated rind of 1 lemon, and 3 tablespoons olive oil. Sprinkle with the fish, season to taste, and cook in a preheated oven, at 425°F, for 15 minutes, until cooked through. Serve with crusty bread.

30 Smoked Haddock and Watercress Cannelloni

Serves 4

butter, for greasing

12 oz skinless smoked haddock
  fillet, cut into pieces

1¼ cups boiling water

10 oz watercress

1 cup crème fraîche

8 fresh lasagna sheets

½ cup dried bread crumbs

salt and black pepper

- Lightly grease an ovenproof dish. Place the haddock in a bowl, pour over the measured water, and let sit for 3 minutes. Drain, reserving the water, and break up the fish.

- Place the watercress in a colander and pour boiling water over it until wilted. Place on a sheet of paper towels and squeeze away excess water, then coarsely chop. Mix with the haddock and 2 tablespoons of the crème fraîche.

- Divide the haddock mixture among the lasagne sheets, arranging it in strip down the middle. Roll up and arrange snugly, seam side down, in the ovenproof dish. Mix the remaining crème fraîche with the haddock soaking water, season, and pour over the top.

- Sprinkle the bread crumbs over the pasta, cover the dish with aluminum foil, and place in a preheated oven, at 400°F, for 20 minutes. Remove the foil and cook under a preheated hot broiler until the bread crumbs are golden.

 Smoked Mackerel and Watercress Omelets Lightly beat 5 eggs in a bowl and season to taste. Heat 1 teaspoon olive oil in a small nonstick skillet, add one-quarter of the beaten egg, and cook for 30 seconds, stirring a little with a spatula. Sprinkle with 1 oz flaked smoked mackerel and cook for another 30 seconds, until just set. Sprinkle with a handful of chopped watercress, fold over, and serve. Repeat with the remaining mixture to make another 3 omelets.

 Smoked Haddock and Watercress Soup Heat 1 tablespoon olive oil in a large, heavy saucepan. Add 1 chopped onion and cook gently for 5 minutes, then add 1 finely diced potato, 3 cups vegetable stock, and 2 smoked haddock fillets. Simmer for 7 minutes, then remove the haddock and flake into chunks. Cook the soup for another 5 minutes, until the potato is just soft, then add 7 oz watercress and ¼ cup heavy cream. Use a handheld immersion blender to puree the soup until smooth, season with black pepper, then return the haddock to the soup and serve.

10 Seared Tuna with Lemon, Bean, and Arugula Salad

Serves 4

1 tablespoon olive oil
4 tuna steaks
2–¼ cup lemon juice
finely grated rind of ½ lemon
3 tablespoons extra virgin olive oil
2 (15 oz) cans cannellini beans,
 rinsed and drained
5 cups arugula
1 small red onion, finely sliced
1 red chile, seeded and chopped
salt and black pepper

- Rub the olive oil over the tuna steaks and season well. Heat a ridged grill pan until smoking hot, then cook the tuna for 1–2 minutes on each side, until seared on the outside but still pink in the middle.

- Meanwhile, mix 2 tablespoons of the lemon juice with the extra virgin olive oil and season to taste. Toss with the remaining ingredients and add more lemon juice, if required. Serve the bean salad with the seared tuna.

---

 2 Lemony Tuna, Bean, and Arugula Gratin Mix 1 cup crème fraîche with ¼ cup boiling water and the finely grated rind of 1 lemon. Add 2 (15 oz) cans cannellini beans, rinsed and drained, 1 (5 oz) can chunk light tuna in oil, drained, and 2 cups chopped arugula. Season to taste, place in an ovenproof dish, and sprinkle with ¾ cup dried bread crumbs mixed with 2 tablespoons finely grated Parmesan cheese. Place in a preheated oven, at 400°F, for 15 minutes, until golden and bubbling.

 3 Creamy Tuna and Bean Risotto with Lemon and Arugula Heat 2 tablespoons olive oil in a large, heavy saucepan. Add 1 finely chopped onion and cook for 5 minutes, until softened, then stir in 1⅓ cups risotto rice, followed by ¼ cup dry white wine, and simmer until boiled away. Gradually add 2½ cups hot vegetable stock, a ladleful at a time, stirring continuously and allowing each ladleful to be absorbed before adding the next. After 15 minutes, add 1 cup rinsed and drained, canned cannellini beans and cook for another 3–5 minutes, until the rice is tender. Stir in 1 (5 oz) can chunk light tuna in oil, drained, and ½ cup finely grated Parmesan cheese. Season to taste, spoon into bowls, and serve topped with the finely grated rind of ½ lemon and a handful of chopped arugula leaves.

ONE-FISH-FUV

30 Oven-Baked Fish and Chips with Tomato Salsa

Serves 4

1½ lb potatoes, cut into thin slices
¼ cup olive oil
4 skinless cod or haddock fillets
Finely grated rind of 1 lemon
1 teaspoon balsamic vinegar
4 tomatoes, chopped
1 teaspoon capers, rinsed
   and drained
1 scallion, chopped
salt and black pepper
handful of chopped parsley,
   to garnish

- Toss the potatoes with half the olive oil, season well, and arrange in a shallow roasting pan. Place in a preheated oven, at 425°F, for 10 minutes.

- Turn over the potatoes, place the fish on top, season again, and sprinkle with the lemon rind. Return to the oven for another 15–20 minutes, until the potatoes are just cooked through.

- Meanwhile, mix the remaining oil with the vinegar, season to taste, and stir in the tomatoes, capers, and scallion. Serve the fish sprinkled with the parsley, with the potatoes and salsa on the side.

 Broiled Fish with Polenta Chips

Brush 3 tablespoons olive oil over 4 skinless cod fillets and 1 lb Italian-style polenta log, thinly sliced. Season to taste and cook under a preheated hot broiler for 5 minutes. Turn the polenta chips over, sprinkle 8 halved cherry tomatoes into the broiler pan, and cook for another 3 minutes, until the fish is cooked. Sprinkle with chopped basil and serve immediately.

 Fish Sticks with Sweet Potato Fries Toss 2 tablespoons olive oil with 1½ lb sweet potatoes, peeled and cut into thin wedges. Season to taste, place in a shallow roasting pan, and cook in a preheated oven, at 400°F, for 7 minutes. Meanwhile, brush 3 tablespoons mayonnaise over 13 oz skinless cod fillet, cut into sticks. Finely grate the rind of 1 lemon and mix with ¾ cup dried bread crumbs on a plate. Toss the fish in the crumbs until coated. Place in the roasting pan and return to the oven for another 10 minutes, until cooked through.

1 Shrimp Salad with Peanut Sauce

Serves 4

8 oz dried thin rice noodles
⅓ cup chunky peanut butter
1 tablespoon sweet chili sauce
2 tablespoons soy sauce
¼ cup boiling water
8 oz cooked, peeled
   large shrimp
½ iceberg lettuce, shredded
1 large carrot, cut into matchsticks
½ cucumber, cut into matchsticks
2 scallions, shredded

- Soak the rice noodles according to the package directions. Mix the peanut butter with the chili sauce, soy sauce, and measured water until smooth.

- Drain the noodles, cool under cold running water, and drain again. Toss with the remaining ingredients, season with salt and black pepper, then drizzle with the sauce to serve.

 2 **Egg-Fried Rice with Shrimp and Peanuts** Heat a wok or large skillet until smoking hot. Add 1 tablespoon vegetable oil and swirl around the wok. Add 2 beaten eggs, stir around for 2 minutes, until set, then remove from the wok and set aside. Add another tablespoon oil to the wok, then add 7 oz peeled, large shrimp. Cook for 3–5 minutes, until pink, then remove from the wok and set aside. Heat another tablespoon oil, add 1 finely chopped shallot, and cook for 2 minutes to soften. Stir in 1 crushed garlic clove and 2 teaspoons finely grated fresh ginger root. Cook for 1 minute, then add 2 cups cooked rice and ½ cup bean sprouts. Stir around the wok, then add the egg and shrimp. Mix together 2 tablespoons lime juice, 2 tablespoons peanut butter, and 2 tablespoons soy sauce and pour into the work. Stir well, then serve topped with chopped fresh cilantro and a handful of chopped roasted peanuts.

3 **Shrimp and Peanut Curry** Heat 1 tablespoon vegetable oil in a casserole dish and add 1 tablespoon Thai red curry paste. Cook over low heat for about 5 minutes, until the oil starts to separate. Stir in 2 tablespoons peanut butter, then add 1¾ cups coconut milk and bring to a boil. Add 2 lime leaves, 1 lemon grass stalk, 1 tablespoon Thai fish sauce, and 1 teaspoon sugar and simmer for 10 minutes. Add 1 sliced red bell pepper and cook for 2 minutes, then stir in 10 baby corn and cook for another 2 minutes. Add 8 oz peeled, large shrimp and cook for 5 minutes, until cooked through. Sprinkle with chopped fresh cilantro.

Spicy Seafood Pasta with Garlic Mayonnaise

Serves 4

2 tablespoons olive oil

1 onion, finely chopped

3 garlic cloves, crushed

½ teaspoon fennel seeds

1 teaspoon smoked paprika

8 oz angel hair pasta, broken into
1¼ inch lengths

1 (14 oz) can diced tomatoes

3 cups hot fish stock

4 oz prepared squid, cut into rings

8 oz mussels, scrubbed, rinsed,
and drained

4 oz raw, peeled shrimp

⅓ cup mayonnaise

salt and black pepper

handful of chopped parsley,
to garnish

- Heat the oil in a large skillet. Add the onion and cook for 5 minutes, until soft, then add 2 of the garlic cloves and cook for another 1 minute. Stir in the fennel seeds, paprika, and pasta and stir for 1 minute, until coated.

- Pour in the tomatoes and stock, season, and bring to a boil. Simmer for 10 minutes, then add the squid, mussels, and shrimp and cook for 3–5 minutes, until the seafood is cooked through, discarding any mussels that don't open.

- Meanwhile, mix the mayonnaise with the remaining garlic. Serve with the pasta, sprinkled with the parsley.

Quick Spicy Seafood Spaghetti

Cook 1 lb fresh spaghetti according to the package directions, then drain and return to the saucepan. Add 1 small crushed garlic clove, 2 chopped tomatoes, 1 chopped chile, 4 oz cooked, peeled shrimp, 4 oz cooked, shelled mussels, and 2 tablespoons olive oil. Squeeze a little lemon juice over the seafood, add a handful of chopped parsley, season to taste, then toss together and serve.

Spanish Seafood Rice

Heat 2 tablespoons olive oil in a deep skillet with a lid. Add 10 oz monkfish, cut into thin slices, and cook for 2 minutes on each side until golden, then remove from the skillet and set aside. Add 1 finely chopped onion to the skillet and cook for 1 minute, then stir in 2 crushed garlic cloves. Add 2 teaspoons tomato paste and 1½ cups paella rice or risotto rice, stir well, and add 3 cups hot fish stock and a pinch of saffron threads. Let simmer for 10 minutes, then add 10 oz clams, rinsed and drained, and 5 oz peeled shrimp. Cover and steam for 5 minutes, until the clams have opened, discarding any that have not. Return the monkfish to the skillet and continue to cook for a few minutes, until the rice and fish are cooked through. Serve with lemon wedges.

ONE-FISH-HUO

30 Cod with Creamy Chowder Sauce

Serves 4

1 tablespoon vegetable oil

4 smoked bacon slices, chopped

1 tablespoon butter

2 leeks, sliced

1 tablespoon all-purpose flour

3 cups fish stock

1 cup milk

3 potatoes, diced

4 cod fillets

½ cup heavy cream

salt and black pepper

handful of chopped chives,
 to garnish

- Heat the oil in a large, heavy saucepan. Add the bacon and cook for 5 minutes, until crisp, then remove from the pan and set aside. Add the butter and leeks to the pan and cook for 3–5 minutes, until softened.

- Stir in the flour, then gradually add the stock and milk, stirring continuously to prevent any lumps from forming. Bring to a boil, add the potatoes, and simmer for 7 minutes.

- Arrange the cod fillets in the pan and cook for another 7 minutes, until they are cooked through. Transfer the cod to warm, shallow serving bowls.

- Stir the cream and most of the bacon into the sauce and season to taste. Warm through and ladle around the fish. Serve sprinkled with chives and the remaining bacon.

10 Smoked Cod with Cream and Spinach

Place 4 smoked cod fillets in a saucepan. Add 1¼ cups hot fish or vegetable stock, bring to a boil, reduce the heat, and simmer for 5–7 minutes, until the fish flakes. Remove the fish and keep warm. Meanwhile, mix ½ cup crème fraîche with 1 egg yolk. Stir in ¼ cup of the poaching liquid, then return to the pan and gently heat until it thickens a little. Place 1 (5 oz) package spinach in a strainer and pour boiling water over it until wilted. Arrange on warm plates and top with the cod. Add a little lemon juice and black pepper to the sauce and pour over the fish.

20 Creamy Smoked Cod and Corn

Chowder Heat 1 tablespoon each vegetable oil and butter in a saucepan. Add 1 finely chopped onion and cook for 5 minutes, until softened. Add 4 cups fish or chicken stock and 1 cup milk and bring to a boil. Add 12 oz new potatoes, halved, and simmer for 7 minutes, then add 10 oz smoked cod fillets and cook for another 5 minutes. Transfer the fish to a plate, remove any skin and bones, and break it into large flakes. Return to the soup with 1 cup frozen corn kernels and ½ cup heavy cream. Heat through, season with pepper, and serve sprinkled with chopped parsley.

20 Hash Browns with Smoked Salmon and Arugula

Serves 4

1½ lb waxy potatoes, coarsely grated

1 small onion, coarsely grated

4 tablespoons butter

3 tablespoons olive oil

2 tablespoons lemon juice

5 cups arugula

8 oz smoked salmon

salt and black pepper

lemon wedges, to serve

- Place the potatoes and onion in a clean dish towel and squeeze to remove excess moisture. Season well. Heat the butter and 1 tablespoon of the oil in a nonstick skillet.

- Add the potato mixture and spread out to make an even layer, then cook for about 10 minutes, until golden. Invert the potatoes onto a plate, then carefully slide back into the skillet the other way up to cook the other side. Cook for another 5–8 minutes, until cooked through and golden all over.

- Meanwhile, mix the lemon juice with the remaining oil and toss with the arugula. Cut the hash brown into wedges and serve with slices of smoked salmon, the arugula salad, and lemon wedges.

 Smoked Salmon and Arugula Pasta

Cook 1 lb fresh penne in a large saucepan of lightly salted boiling water according to the package directions. Drain and return to the pan. Add ¼ cup crème fraîche, 2 tablespoons lemon juice, and 6 oz smoked salmon, cut into strips. Toss through 4 cups arugula and season to taste just before serving.

 Roasted Salmon and Potatoes with Arugula Dressing Toss 1½ lb halved new potatoes with 3 tablespoons olive oil and place in a roasting pan. Season to taste and cook in a preheated oven, at 400°F, for 15 minutes, turning once during cooking. Arrange 4 salmon fillets in the pan with the potatoes, season to taste, then return to the oven for

another 12–15 minutes, until the fish and potatoes are cooked through. Meanwhile, mix 1 (5 oz) package arugula, chopped, with 1 tablespoon capers, rinsed and drained, the finely grated rind and juice of ½ lemon, and 3 tablespoons olive oil. Spoon the dressing over the salmon and potatoes before serving.

QuickCook

Meat

Recipes listed by cooking time

30

20

10

30 Roasted Sausages with Parsnips and Carrots

Serves 4

8 pork sausages
1 onion, cut into wedges
2 large carrots, cut into wedges
2 large parsnips, cut into wedges
4 garlic cloves, unpeeled
2 tablespoons olive oil
1 teaspoon honey
handful of rosemary sprigs
salt and black pepper

- Place the sausages, onion, carrots, parsnips, and garlic in a large, shallow roasting pan. Toss together with the oil and season to taste.

- Place in a preheated oven, at 400°F, for 20 minutes, giving the pan a good shake halfway through cooking. Drizzle with the honey and rosemary, then return to the oven for another 5–10 minutes, until golden and cooked through.

 Creamy Parsnip and Prosciutto Pasta

Cook 1 sliced parsnip in a large saucepan of lightly salted boiling water for 5 minutes, then add 1 lb fresh tagliatelle and cook according to the package directions until tender. Drain and return the pasta and parsnip to the pan. Stir in ⅓ cup crème fraîche or heavy cream and 4 slices of prosciutto, cut into strips. Season to taste and serve sprinkled with thyme leaves.

 Carrot, Parsnip, and Sausage Minestrone Heat 1 tablespoon olive oil in a large, heavy saucepan. Add 1 finely chopped onion, 1 chopped carrot, and 1 chopped parsnip and cook for 5 minutes, until softened. Stir in 1 crushed garlic clove, 1 tablespoon tomato paste, 6 cups chicken stock, and a pinch of dried rosemary and simmer for 5 minutes. Add 1½ cups shredded kale, 1 cup rinsed and drained, canned cannellini beans, and 4 thickly sliced kabanos or other smoked sausages. Season to taste and simmer for another 5 minutes or until cooked through, then serve with plenty of crusty bread.

10 Thai Beef Salad with Herbs

Serves 4

⅓ cup Thai fish sauce
finely grated rind and juice of
  ½ lime
2 teaspoons granulated sugar
1 garlic clove, crushed
1 teaspoon finely grated fresh
  ginger root
1 lemon grass stalk, finely chopped
1 red chile, finely chopped
handful of chopped fresh cilantro
handful of chopped mint
1 tablespoon vegetable oil
1 lb top sirloin or tenderloin steak
2 cups cherry tomatoes
½ cucumber, thinly sliced
handful of salad greens

- Mix together the fish sauce, lime rind and juice, and sugar until the sugar dissolves, then stir in the garlic, ginger, lemon grass, chile, and herbs to make a dressing.

- Rub the oil over the steak and season to taste. Cook in a smoking hot grill pan for 2–3 minutes on each side, then remove from the pan and cut into slices.

- Place the quartered tomatoes, cucumber, and salad greens on a serving plate, arrange the warm beef on top, and drizzle with the dressing. Serve immediately.

 Thai Beef and Rice with Herbs Heat 1 tablespoon oil in a nonstick skillet. Add 2 thinly sliced top sirloin steaks and cook for 1 minute on each side. Set aside. Add more oil to the skillet, then cook 1 finely chopped onion for 5 minutes. Stir in 2 teaspoons grated ginger root, 2 crushed garlic cloves, and 8 cherry tomatoes. Cook for 5 minutes, then add 3 tablespoons Thai fish sauce and 1 teaspoon sugar. Stir in a handful of chopped basil and fresh cilantro, add 2 cups cooked rice, and heat through. Return the beef to the skillet and heat through. Serve with chili sauce.

 Thai Beef Lettuce Cups with Herbs Mix 2 tablespoons Thai fish sauce with ½ chopped red chile and 1 finely chopped lemon grass stalk. Rub all over 3 top sirloin or tenderloin steaks and set aside to marinate for 20 minutes. Heat a skillet until smoking hot. Add 1 tablespoon oil, then cook 1 cored, seeded, and sliced red bell pepper for 1–2 minutes, until lightly browned. Remove from the skillet and set aside. Add the steaks to the skillet, cook for 2–3 minutes on each side, then cut into thick slices. Add the remaining marinate to the skillet with another tablespoon fish sauce, a pinch of brown sugar, and a little water. Heat until bubbly and syrupy. Break 2 Boston lettuce into separate leaves and arrange on plates. Place a little chopped cucumber into each leaf, then pile the red bell pepper and beef on top. Drizzle with the sauce and top with a handful of fresh cilantro and mint leaves to serve.

30 Pork and Tomato Rice with Spinach

Serves 4

3 tablespoons olive oil
10 oz pork tenderloin, sliced
1 onion, finely chopped
3 garlic cloves, finely chopped
1⅓ cups paella rice or risotto rice
2 teaspoons smoked paprika
¾ cup can diced tomatoes
2¾ cups hot chicken stock
4 cups baby spinach leaves
salt and black pepper
lemon wedges, to serve

- Heat 1 tablespoon of the oil in a large, deep skillet over high heat. Add the pork tenderloin and cook for 3 minutes, until golden and nearly cooked through, then remove from the skillet and set aside. Reduce the heat, add the onion to the skillet with the remaining oil, and cook for 3 minutes, until softened, then stir in the garlic and cook for 30 seconds.

- Add the rice and cook for 1 minute, then add the paprika and tomatoes, bring to a boil, and simmer for 2–3 minutes. Pour in the stock, season to taste, and cook for another 12–15 minutes, until there is just a little liquid left around the edges of the skillet.

- Lightly fork the spinach through the rice, arrange the pork on top, then cover and continue to cook for 3–4 minutes, until cooked through. Serve with lemon wedges for squeezing over the dish.

 Spicy Pork and Tomato Fried Rice

Heat 2 tablespoons vegetable oil in a large wok. Add 10 oz pork tenderloin, cut into strips, and stir-fry for 3 minutes, until golden. Stir in 2 sliced garlic cloves and 2 teaspoons finely grated fresh ginger root. Add 2 chopped tomatoes and a pinch of dried red pepper flakes, then add 2 cups cooked rice and a large handful of chopped basil. Season to taste, heat through, and serve immediately.

 Chorizo, Tomato, and Rice Soup

Heat 2 tablespoons olive oil in a large, heavy saucepan. Add 4 oz thickly sliced chorizo, cook for 2–3 minutes, until golden, then add 1 sliced garlic clove. Pour in 1 (14½ oz) can diced tomatoes and 4 cups hot vegetable stock. Add a pinch of sugar, season to taste, and simmer for 10 minutes. Stir in 2 cups cooked rice and 5 cups arugula, heat through, and serve.

 # Melting Meatball Sandwiches

Serves 4

1 tablespoon olive oil

10 oz small store-bought beef meatballs

1½ cups store-bought tomato sauce

4 ciabatta rolls

4 oz mozzarella cheese, sliced

4 cups arugula

salt and black pepper

- Heat the oil in a skillet. Add the meatballs and cook for 5 minutes, until browned all over. Pour in the sauce and bring to a boil, then reduce the heat and simmer for 10 minutes. Taste and adjust the seasoning, if necessary.

- Lightly toast the ciabattas and split in half. Pile the meatballs and sauce on the bottom halves, top with the mozzarella, and cook under a preheated hot broiler for 1–2 minutes, until starting to melt. Add some arugula, replace the ciabatta tops, and serve immediately.

 ### Italian Steak Sandwiches

Lightly toast 4 large slices of ciabatta bread in a smoking hot ridged grill pan. Rub 1 tablespoon olive oil over 4 top sirloin steaks, season well, and cook in the grill pan for 2–3 minutes on each side, until just cooked through. Arrange the steaks on the bread and top with a handful of cherry tomatoes, 4 cups arugula, and some Parmesan cheese shavings.

 ### Sloppy Joe Sandwiches

Heat 2 tablespoons oil in a deep skillet. Add 12 oz ground beef and cook for 5 minutes, until starting to turn brown. Add 1 chopped onion and cook for another 5 minutes, until softened. Stir in 1 crushed garlic clove, a pinch of chili powder, and ¼ cup store-bought barbecue sauce. Pour in 1 (14½ oz) can diced tomatoes and 1 cored, seeded, and chopped red bell pepper, season, and simmer for 15 minutes. Split 4 burger buns and spoon some of the mixture inside. Top with shredded cheddar cheese and sliced iceberg lettuce.

ONE-MEAT-PIA

20 Lamb with Eggplant and Tomato Salad

Serves 4

1/3 cup olive oil
4 baby eggplants, halved
1/2 teaspoon ground cumin
1/2 teaspoon smoked paprika
2 garlic cloves, crushed
finely grated rind and juice of
  1/2 lemon
handful of chopped fresh cilantro
3 tomatoes, chopped
8 lamb chops
salt and black pepper

- Rub 2 tablespoons of the oil over the eggplant slices and season well. Heat a ridged grill pan until smoking hot, then cook the eggplant for about 5 minutes, until soft and lightly charred all over.

- Mix the spices, garlic, lemon rind and juice, and cilantro with 3 tablespoons of the oil, season to taste, and toss with the tomatoes and warm eggplant.

- Rub the remaining oil over the lamb and season to taste. Cook in the ridged grill pan for 3–5 minutes on each side until golden on the outside and still just pink in the middle. Serve with the tomato and eggplant salad.

 Grilled Lamb with Eggplant Puree
Drizzle 1 tablespoon olive oil over 8 lamb chops and season to taste. Cook in a smoking hot ridged grill pan for 3–5 minutes on each side until browned on the outside and still pink in the middle. Meanwhile, remove the skin from 8 oz of roasted eggplant from a jar, and place in a food processor with 1/4 cup plain yogurt and a handful of chopped fresh cilantro. Season to taste, blend until smooth, and serve with the chops and some crusty bread.

 Lamb and Eggplant Moussaka Heat 3 tablespoons olive oil in a flameproof skillet. Add 1 sliced eggplant and cook for 5 minutes, until softened and golden. Remove from the skillet and season to taste. Add more oil to the skillet, if necessary, then cook 1 finely chopped onion and 10 oz ground lamb for 5–10 minutes, until softened and golden. Stir in 2 crushed garlic cloves, a pinch of ground cinnamon, and 1 tablespoon tomato paste. Add 1 (14 1/2 oz) can diced tomatoes, season to taste, and simmer for 10 minutes. Arrange the eggplant slices on top of the meat mixture, then spoon 1 beaten egg mixed with 2/3 cup plain yogurt over the top. Sprinkle 1/4 cup grated Parmesan cheese on top and cook under a preheated hot broiler for 5 minutes, until the topping is set and golden.

ONE-MEAT-LOX

30 Beef Stew with Garlic Bread Topping

Serves 4

2 tablespoons olive oil

13 oz chuck steak, cut into chunks

1 onion, sliced

1 carrot, sliced

1 celery stick, sliced

1 teaspoon tomato paste

2 teaspoons all-purpose flour

handful of chopped thyme

½ cup red wine

1 cup hot beef stock

½ store-bought garlic bread baguette, sliced

salt and black pepper

- Heat half the oil in a flameproof casserole dish over high heat. Add the beef and cook for 2–3 minutes, until golden, then remove from the dish and set aside. Add the remaining oil and cook the onion, carrot, and celery for 5 minutes, until softened.

- Stir in the tomato paste, flour, and thyme, then pour in the wine and cook for 2–3 minutes, until reduced by half. Add the stock and simmer for 15 minutes, then return the meat to the dish.

- Arrange the garlic bread slices on top of the stew, then cook under a preheated hot broiler for 3 minutes, until the bread is golden and crisp.

---

10 Steaks with Garlic Butter Topping

Mix 4 tablespoons softened butter with 1 crushed garlic clove and 1 tablespoon finely grated Parmesan cheese. Heat a ridged grill pan until smoking hot. Rub 1 tablespoon olive oil over 4 top sirloin steaks and season to taste. Cook in the grill pan for 2–3 minutes on each side, placing a pat of the flavored butter on top of each steak for the last minute of cooking. Serve the steaks in crusty baguettes with a handful of shredded lettuce.

20 Beef Noodles with Garlic Sauce

Heat 1 tablespoon vegetable oil in a wok or large skillet. Add 2 thinly sliced top sirloin steaks, stir-fry for 2–3 minutes, until browned, then remove from the wok and set aside. Add a little more oil and 1 sliced onion to the wok and cook for 2 minutes, until starting to soften, then add 5 oz sliced shiitake mushrooms and cook for another 1 minute. Add 2 sliced garlic cloves and stir-fry until the vegetables are soft. Stir in ⅓ cup oyster sauce and 1 tablespoon soy sauce and simmer for 5 minutes, then add 3 cups baby spinach leaves and 4 oz rice noodles, cooked. Add a splash of water if necessary, return the beef to the pan, and cook until heated through.

3 0 Bacon and Apple Bites

Serves 4

1 tablespoon olive oil, for greasing
1 small onion, sliced
6 bacon slices, chopped
1/3 cup all-purpose flour
1 egg
2/3 cup low-fat milk
2 teaspoons whole-grain mustard
1 Pippin apple, sliced
salt and black pepper

- Liberally grease a 4-cup muffin pan with cups 3½ inches across. Divide the onion and bacon among the cups in the pan and cook in a preheated oven, at 475°F, for 5 minutes.

- Meanwhile, place the flour, egg, milk, and mustard in a blender, season to taste, and blend until smooth.

- Arrange the apple in the cups in the pan, then pour the batter over them. Return to the oven for another 20 minutes or until puffed and golden.

 ### Bacon and Apple Salad

Cook 4 bacon slices and 2 slices of bread under a preheated medium broiler for 5–7 minutes, turning once, until golden and crisp. Break the bacon and bread into large pieces. Mix 1 tablespoon apple vinegar, 1 teaspoon mustard, and 1 teaspoon honey with 3 tablespoons olive oil and season well. Toss the dressing with the bread croutons, 1 (5 oz) package mixed salad greens, and 1 sliced Granny Smith apple. Divide among serving plates, then top with the bacon, ¼ cup shelled walnuts or pecans, and 1/3 cup crumbled goat cheese.

 ### Bacon, Apple, and Celeriac Soup

Heat 1 tablespoon olive oil in a large, heavy saucepan. Add 4 chopped bacon slices and cook for 2 minutes, until golden, then remove from the pan and set aside. Add 1 finely chopped onion to the pan and cook for 2 minutes, then add 1 finely chopped celeriac and 1 small chopped Pippin apple. Cook for another 5 minutes, until softened. Pour in 6 cups hot chicken stock and simmer for 7 minutes or until soft. Use a handheld immersion blender to puree the soup until smooth, then season to taste and stir in ¼ cup crème fraîche or heavy cream. Ladle the soup into bowls and sprinkle with the bacon. Mix ¼ cup crème fraiche or heavy cream with 2 teaspoons whole-grain mustard, then serve with the soup and some toasted sourdough bread.

30 Lamb Stew with Feta and Pasta

Serves 4

2 tablespoons olive oil

12 oz boneless lamb shoulder, cut
   into bite-size pieces

1 onion, sliced

2 garlic cloves, crushed

1 tablespoon tomato paste

½ teaspoon ground cinnamon

pinch of dried red pepper flakes

1 red bell pepper, cored, seeded,
   and sliced

3 cups hot chicken stock

10 oz small soup pasta shapes

salt and black pepper

3 tablespoons crumbed feta
   cheese

handful of chopped parsley,
   to garnish

- Heat the oil in a large flameproof casserole dish. Add the lamb and cook for 5 minutes, until starting to brown, then add the onion and cook for another 7–8 minutes, until soft. Stir in the garlic, tomato paste, spices, and red bell pepper, then pour in the stock.

- Bring to a boil, then reduce the heat and simmer for 1–2 minutes. Add the pasta and cook for 12 minutes, or according to the package directions, until the pasta is tender and most of the liquid has boiled away. Season to taste, then serve sprinkled with the feta and parsley.

10 Lamb and Feta Pockets

Mix 1 tablespoon olive oil with a pinch of dried oregano and the finely grated rind of 1 lemon, then rub over 12 oz cubed lamb. Season to taste and cook in a smoking hot ridged grill pan for 5–7 minutes, turning frequently, until lightly browned. Serve in pita breads with a handful of shredded romaine lettuce, sliced cucumber, and halved cherry tomatoes. Drizzle with lemon juice and olive oil, then top with 3 tablespoons crumbled feta cheese, 1 chopped red chile, and more dried oregano.

20 Broiled Lamb with Feta and Couscous

Rub 1 tablespoon olive oil all over 8 lamb chops, arrange in a roasting pan, and season. Cook under a preheated hot broiler for 4 minutes on each side. Sprinkle 1½ cups couscous into the pan and pour in 1½ cups hot chicken stock. Cover tightly with aluminum foil and let rest for 5 minutes, until the couscous is tender. Transfer the chops to serving plates. Fluff up the couscous with a fork and stir in the juice of 1 lemon, a handful of chopped oregano, 1 chopped red chile, ½ cup pitted ripe black olives, and ⅓ cup crumbled feta cheese. Serve the couscous with the chops.

Prosciutto and Asparagus Tart

Serves 4

butter, for greasing
1 sheet ready-to-bake
   puff pastry
1 egg, beaten
⅔ cup ricotta cheese
¼ cup grated Parmesan cheese
5 oz fine asparagus spears
4 slices of prosciutto
salt and black pepper

- Place the pastry on a baking sheet and use a sharp knife to score a ½ inch border around the edges, making sure you don't cut all the way through the pastry. Prick all over the center of the pastry using a fork.

- Mix together the ricotta, Parmesan, and the remaining beaten egg and season well. Spoon the mixture over the tart, making sure it doesn't spread outside the border. Arrange the asparagus on top. Place in a preheated oven, at 425°F, for 12 minutes.

- Arrange the prosciutto on top of the tart and return to the oven for 5–7 minutes, until the pastry is puffed and cooked through.

Crispy Prosciutto, Asparagus, and Arugula Salad Cut 5 prosciutto slices into long strips and wrap around 4 oz fine asparagus spears. Drizzle with olive oil and season well with black pepper. Cook under a preheated hot broiler for 5 minutes, turning once, until golden and crisp. Beat 1 tablespoon balsamic vinegar with 3 tablespoons olive oil and season. Toss the dressing with 1 (5 oz) package arugula and divide among serving plates. Arrange the prosciutto-wrapped asparagus spears around the arugula, then sprinkle ⅓ cup crumbled goat cheese on top.

Prosciutto and Asparagus Frittata Heat 3 tablespoons olive oil in a flameproof nonstick skillet. Add 1 sliced potato and cook for 7 minutes, until starting to soften, then add 4 oz asparagus tips and cook for another 5 minutes, until the potatoes and asparagus are tender. Beat 6 eggs with ¼ cup finely grated Parmesan, season to taste, and pour into the skillet. Cook over gentle heat for 15 minutes, until the eggs are nearly set. Arrange 4 slices of prosciutto on top and cook under a preheated hot broiler for 2–3 minutes, until set. Sprinkle with a handful of chopped basil before serving.

ONE-MEAT-KIW

Stir-Fried Teriyaki Beef with Noodles and Greens

Serves 4

2 tablespoons vegetable oil

12 oz tenderloin steak, cut into strips

2 garlic cloves, sliced

1 teaspoon finely grated fresh ginger root

2 cups chopped collard greens

4 oz udon noodles, cooked

¼ cup teriyaki sauce

1 tablespoon sesame seeds

- Heat the oil in a large wok or skillet. Add the beef strips and cook for 1 minute, until browned, then remove from the wok and set aside.

- Add the garlic, ginger, and greens to the wok and stir-fry for 2–3 minutes, until the greens start to wilt.

- Return the beef to the wok, add the noodles and teriyaki sauce, then cook, adding a little boiling water if necessary, until heated through. Sprinkle with the sesame seeds and serve immediately.

Simple Braised Teriyaki Beef

Heat 1 tablespoon oil in a flameproof casserole dish. Add 2 sliced onions and cook over low heat for 10 minutes, until golden. Add ½ cup hot beef stock, 3 tablespoons soy sauce, 2 tablespoons rice wine or dry sherry, and 1 tablespoon granulated sugar. Simmer for 1–2 minutes, then add 1 cup chopped collard greens and cook for another 2 minutes. Stir in 12 oz thinly sliced top sirloin steak and cook for 3 minutes, until just cooked. Sprinkle with 1 sliced red chile before serving with boiled rice, if desired.

Marinated Teriyaki Beef with Spinach and Radish Salad

Mix 2 teaspoons finely grated fresh ginger root with ⅓ cup teriyaki sauce. Pour over 4 top sirloin steaks and let marinate for 20 minutes. Meanwhile, mix 1 tablespoon light miso paste with 3 tablespoons teriyaki sauce, 1 teaspoon finely grated fresh ginger root, 1 teaspoon sesame oil, and a little water to make a dressing. Toss with ¾ cup thinly sliced radishes and 3½ cups baby spinach leave,s then sprinkle with 1 tablespoon sesame seeds. Remove the steaks from the marinade, brush with 1 tablespoon vegetable oil, and cook in a preheated hot ridged grill pan for 2–3 minutes on each side, until just cooked through. Let rest for a couple of minutes, then cut into thick slices and serve with the salad.

20 Chorizo and Black Bean Soup

Serves 4

2 tablespoons vegetable oil
1 onion, finely chopped
4 oz chorizo, finely diced
1 red bell pepper, cored, seeded, and chopped
1 garlic clove, chopped
1 teaspoon ground cumin
6 cups hot chicken stock
2 (15 oz) cans black beans, rinsed and drained
salt and black pepper
2 tablespoons lime juice
¼ cup sour cream
handful of chopped fresh cilantro leaves
1 red chile, chopped

- Heat the oil in a large, heavy saucepan. Add the onion, chorizo, red bell pepper, and garlic and cook for 7–10 minutes, until soft, then stir in the cumin. Pour in the stock and beans and simmer for 5–8 minutes.

- Season to taste, then use a potato masher to roughly mash some of the beans to thicken the soup. Ladle the soup into bowls and squeeze a little lime juice over each serving. Add a spoonful of sour cream, top with a sprinkling of cilantro and chile, and serve immediately.

 Chorizo and Black Bean Salad

Rinse and drain 1 (15 oz) can black beans. Mix with 2 tablespoons extra virgin olive oil and a good squeeze of lime juice. Season to taste and add 2 chopped tomatoes, 2 chopped scallions, and a good handful of chopped fresh cilantro. Place on a serving plate and arrange slices of fried chorizo on top. Serve with crusty bread.

 Chorizo, Black Bean, and Sweet Potato Chile Heat 1 tablespoon vegetable oil in a large, heavy saucepan. Add 1 finely chopped onion and 3 oz chopped chorizo and cook for 5 minutes to soften. Add 1 teaspoon ground cumin, 1 teaspoon smoked paprika, and 1 peeled and diced sweet potato, stir well, and pour in 1 (14½ oz) can diced tomatoes and 1 cup water. Simmer for 15 minutes, then add 1 (15 oz) can black beans, rinsed and drained. Season to taste and cook for another 3–5 minutes, until heated through, then serve topped with spoonfuls of sour cream and sprinkled with chopped fresh cilantro.

30 Lamb and Pomegranate Pilaf

Serves 4

1 tablespoon vegetable oil
12 oz boneless lamb shoulder,
 cut into chunks
1 onion, finely chopped
1 garlic clove, finely chopped
½ teaspoon ground cinnamon
pinch of allspice
1½ cups long grain rice
finely grated rind and juice of
 1 orange
3½ cups chicken stock
½ cup halved dried figs
¼ cup shelled pistachio nuts
handful of fresh chopped mint
handful of fresh chopped parsley
seeds from ½ pomegranate
salt and black pepper

- Heat the oil in a large flameproof casserole dish. Add the lamb and cook for 2–3 minutes, until browned all over. Add the onion and cook for 5 minutes, until softened, then stir in the garlic, cinnamon, and allspice. Add the rice and stir until coated.

- Add the orange rind and juice to the dish, followed by the chicken stock and figs, then season to taste. Bring to a boil, then reduce the heat and simmer for 12 minutes, until most of the stock has been absorbed.

- Cover tightly and cook over low heat for another 5 minutes, until the rice is cooked through. Use a fork to gently stir in the pistachios, herbs, and pomegranate seeds, then serve immediately.

 Pomegranate-Glazed Lamb Chops with Salad Mix 2 tablespoons pomegranate molasses with a squeeze of lemon juice and pinch of dried red pepper flakes. Rub all over 8 large lamb chops. Cook under a preheated hot broiler for 3–4 minutes on each side, until browned and just cooked through. Mix 3 tablespoons orange juice with 3 tablespoons olive oil, season, and toss with 1 (5 oz) package salad greens and 4 quartered figs. Sprinkle the salad with ⅓ cup crumbled feta cheese and serve with the chops.

 Bulgur Pilaf with Lamb Sausages and Pomegranate Heat 1 tablespoon olive oil in a deep skillet. Add 12 oz lamb sausages and cook until browned all over, then add 1 crushed garlic clove, 1 chopped red chile, a pinch of ground cinnamon, and 1½ cups bulgur wheat. Stir in the finely grated rind and juice of 1 orange and 1 cup hot chicken stock. Simmer for 10 minutes, until the sausages are cooked through and the bulgur is tender. Remove the sausages from the skillet and cut into thick slices.

Lightly fork a handful of chopped mint and parsley into the pilaf, sprinkle with shelled pistachio nuts and pomegranate seeds, and serve with the sausages.

1⏱ Creamy Ham and Tomato Penne

Serves 4

1 lb fresh penne pasta
½ cup frozen peas
½ cup crème fraîche or
   heavy cream
4 slices of ham, torn into
   bite-size pieces
8 cherry tomatoes, halved
4 cups arugula
salt and black pepper

- Cook the penne in a large saucepan of lightly salted boiling water according to the package directions. Add the frozen peas for the final minute of cooking.

- Drain and return the pasta and peas to the pan, stir in the remaining ingredients, and season to taste. Serve immediately.

2⏱ Creamy Ham and Tomato Soup

Heat 1 tablespoon olive oil in a large, heavy saucepan. Add 1 chopped onion and cook for 5 minutes, until softened, then add 1 (14½ oz) can diced tomatoes, a pinch of sugar, and a handful of chopped basil. Simmer for 12 minutes, then use a handheld immersion blender to puree the soup until smooth. Add a little boiling water if it is too thick. Stir in 4 oz chopped ham and ⅓ cup crème fraîche or heavy cream, season to taste, heat through, and serve with crusty bread.

3⏱ Pork and Tomato Stew with Creamy Mascarpone

Heat 1 tablespoon olive oil in a flameproof casserole dish over high heat. Cook 12 oz pork tenderloin, cut into thick strips, for 3–5 minutes, until golden. You may have to do this in 2 batches. Remove from the dish and set aside. Add 1 chopped onion to the dish and cook for 3 minutes. Stir in 2 crushed garlic cloves and 1 chopped fennel bulb and cook for another 2–3 minutes, until softened. Pour in ½ cup dry white wine and bring to a boil. Add 1 (14½ oz) can plum tomatoes and 10 oz small new potatoes and simmer for 12 minutes, until the potatoes are tender, then return the pork to the dish, heat through, and season to taste. Mix 3 tablespoons mascarpone cheese with a handful of chopped basil, 1 crushed garlic clove, and 1 teaspoon finely grated lemon rind. Serve the stew topped with spoonfuls of the mascarpone.

Seared Pork Chops with Chile Corn

Serves 4

2 tablespoons olive oil

4 pork chops

1⅓ cups fresh or canned
   corn kernels

2 scallions, thinly sliced

1 red chile, chopped

⅓ cup crème fraîche or
   Greek yogurt

finely grated rind of 1 lime

salt and black pepper

handful of chopped fresh cilantro
   leaves

- Heat a large skillet, add half the oil, and swirl around the pan. Season the chops to taste and cook in the skillet for 5–7 minutes on each side, until golden and cooked through. Remove from the skillet and keep warm.

- Add the remaining oil to the skillet, followed by the corn. Cook for 2 minutes, until starting to brown, then stir in the scallions and chile and cook for another 1 minute. Add the crème fraîche or Greek yogurt and lime rind and season to taste. Sprinkle with the cilantro and serve with the pork chops.

 Ham and Corn Melts

Spread ½ cup cream cheese over 4 wheat tortillas. Tear up 4 slices of ham and sprinkle on top with ½ cup canned corn kernels and ¼ cup shredded cheddar cheese. Place another tortilla on top of each, then cook under a preheated broiler for 3 minutes. Carefully turn over and cook for another 2–3 minutes, until the cheese has melted inside.

 Bacon and Chile Cornbread

Heat 2 tablespoons vegetable oil and 4 tablespoons butter in an ovenproof skillet. Add 1 finely chopped onion and 4 chopped bacon slices and cook for about 3 minutes, until softened, then stir in 1 finely chopped red chile. Meanwhile, place 1½ cups cornmeal in a food processor with 1¼ cups all-purpose flour, 1 tablespoon sugar, 2 teaspoons baking powder, 1 teaspoon salt, 2⅓ cups buttermilk, and 1 egg and blend until smooth. Stir in the onions and bacon, then pour the batter to the skillet and sprinkle ½ cup shredded cheddar cheese on top. Bake in a preheated oven, at 450°F, for 25 minutes, until just cooked through.

Moroccan Lamb Stew

Serves 4

1 tablespoon olive oil

½ onion, chopped

2 garlic cloves, crushed

2 teaspoons finely grated fresh ginger root

2 teaspoons ras el hanout spice mix (available in Middle Eastern markets)

1 (14½ oz) can diced tomatoes

4 eggs

salt and black pepper

handful of chopped fresh cilantro

For the meatballs

½ onion, grated

12 oz ground lamb

1 teaspoon ras el hanout spice mix

1 egg yolk

- First make the meatballs. Squeeze the grated onion to get rid of any excess moisture, then mix with the lamb, ras el hanout, and egg yolk and season well. Lightly wet your hands and shape the mixture into 12 meatballs, each about the size of a golf ball.

- Heat the oil in a skillet. Add the meatballs and cook for 5 minutes, until starting to turn golden. Add the chopped onion and cook for 3 minutes, until softened, then add the garlic and ginger and cook for another 1 minute. Stir in the ras el hanout, then pour in the tomatoes. Season to taste and simmer for 12 minutes, topping up with a little water, if necessary.

- Make 4 holes in the mixture and crack an egg into each. Loosely cover the skillet with aluminum foil and simmer for 5 minutes or until the egg whites are just cooked through. Serve sprinkled with the cilantro.

 Moroccan Spiced Lamb Kebabs Mix 2 teaspoons ras el hanout spice mix with 1 tablespoon olive oil and the finely grated rind of 1 lemon. Rub over 12 oz lamb cubes, then thread onto metal skewers. Season to taste and cook under a preheated hot broiler for 5–7 minutes, turning often, until golden and cooked through. Serve in toasted pita breads with some sliced tomatoes and cucumber, a handful of mint leaves, and a drizzle of plain yogurt.

 Moroccan Lamb Chops with Grilled Tomatoes and Beans Mix 2 tablespoons plain yogurt with 1 tablespoon olive oil and 1 teaspoon ras el hanout. Rub over 8 lamb chops and let marinate for 10 minutes. Meanwhile, heat a ridged grill pan until smoking hot. Toss 8 cherry tomatoes in 2 teaspoons olive oil, season, and cook for 2 minutes in the grill pan until lightly browned. Remove and set aside. Cook the lamb chops in the preheated grill pan for 3–5 minutes on each side until lightly brown. Meanwhile, mix 2 (15 oz) cans lima beans, rinsed and drained, with 3 tablespoons olive oil, a good squeeze of lemon juice, a handful each of chopped mint and parsley, and the grilled tomatoes. Serve the chops with the bean salad and a spoonful of plain yogurt.

1 Herbed Steak Tortilla Wraps

Serves 4

2 kaffir lime leaves
1 shallot
1 garlic clove
bunch of basil
handful of oregano
1 tablespoon red wine vinegar
⅓ cup olive oil
1 onion, sliced
4 top sirloin steaks
4 wheat tortillas
⅓ cup plain yogurt
1 red chile, chopped
salt and black pepper

- Place the lime leaves, shallot, garlic, herbs, vinegar, and ¼ cup of the oil in a food processor, blend to form a thick sauce, and season to taste.

- Toss the onion and steaks with the remaining oil and season well. Heat a ridged grill pan until smoking hot, add the onion and steaks, and cook for 2 minutes. Turn the steaks over and move the onions around the pan and cook for another 2–3 minutes, until cooked to your liking. Remove from the pan and keep warm.

- Warm the tortillas through on the grill pan. Cut the steaks into thick slices and divide among the tortillas with the onions. Drizzle with the yogurt and herb sauce, then sprinkle with the chile. Roll up the tortillas neatly and serve immediately.

 Beef Tortilla Wedges

Lay 4 large tortillas on 2 baking sheets. Divide 1 (15 oz) can refried beans between them and spread all over. Cut 5 oz sliced roasted beef into thin strips and sprinkle on top. Add 2 sliced tomatoes, ½ cup shredded cheddar cheese, and 3 oz sliced mozzarella cheese. Sprinkle with chopped fresh cilantro and top each with another tortilla. Place in a preheated oven, at 400°F, for 10 minutes, until golden. Serve cut into wedges.

 Spicy Beef Stew with Tortillas

Heat 1 tablespoon oil in a deep skillet over high heat. Add 12 oz top sirloin steak, cut into strips, and cook for 1–2 minutes on each side, until golden. Remove from the skillet and set aside. Add another tablespoon oil to the skillet with 1 finely chopped onion and 3 oz diced chorizo and cook for 5 minutes, until the onion has softened. Stir in 1 crushed garlic clove, 1 teaspoon ground cumin, and a pinch of ground cinnamon. Add 1 teaspoon tomato paste, then pour in 1 (14½ oz) can diced tomatoes and a pinch of sugar. Simmer for 15 minutes, topping up with water, if necessary. Return the beef to the skillet, season to taste, and heat through. Serve the stew on tortillas, topped with spoonfuls of sour cream, plenty of chopped fresh cilantro, some shredded cheddar cheese, and a squeeze of lime juice.

30 Sausage and Bean Cassoulet

Serves 4

2 tablespoons olive oil
6 pork sausages
1 onion, chopped
2 garlic cloves, chopped
1 (14½ oz) can diced tomatoes
½ cup chicken stock
1 bay leaf
1 (15 oz) can cannellini beans,
  rinsed and drained
1 cup dried bread crumbs
handful of chopped parsley
salt and black pepper

- Heat 1 tablespoon of the oil in a shallow, flameproof casserole dish. Add the sausages and cook for 5 minutes until starting to turn golden, then add the onion and cook for another 5 minutes, until softened.

- Cut the sausages into thick slices, then return to the dish with the garlic and cook for 1 minute. Add the tomatoes, stock, bay leaf, and beans, season to taste, and bring to a boil. Reduce the heat and simmer for 5 minutes.

- Mix together the bread crumbs and thyme and sprinkle over the cassoulet, then drizzle with the remaining oil. Cook in a preheated oven, at 400°F, for 10–12 minutes, until the topping is golden and crisp.

 Warm Chorizo and Bean Salad

Heat 2 tablespoons olive oil in a deep skillet. Add 4 oz sliced thick chorizo sausage and cook for 3 minutes, until starting to turn golden, then add 2 sliced garlic cloves and cook for another 1 minute. Stir in 8 halved cherry tomatoes and cook for 1–2 minutes, until starting to soften. Add 1 (15 oz) can cannellini beans, rinsed and drained, and heat through. Season to taste, sprinkle with chopped parsley, and serve.

 Creamy White Bean and Sausage

Gratin Mix together 4 sliced cooked smoked sausages, 2 (15 oz) cans cannellini beans, rinsed and drained, ½ cup crème fraîche or heavy cream, ⅓ cup hot vegetable stock, and a handful of chopped thyme. Transfer to an ovenproof dish and top with ¾ cup dried bread crumbs and ¼ cup shredded Gruyère or Swiss cheese. Place in a preheated oven, at 425°F, for 15 minutes, until golden and bubbling.

30 Rosemary-Crusted Roasted Lamb

Serves 4

1½ lb small new potatoes, halved
6 small carrots
3 tablespoons olive oil
3 tablespoons Dijon mustard
2 garlic cloves, crushed
2 racks of lamb, 7–8 bones each
1 tablespoon chopped rosemary
½ cup dried bread crumbs
2 teaspoons balsamic vinegar
2 tablespoons red currant jelly
⅓ cup chicken or lamb stock
salt and black pepper

- Toss the potatoes and carrots with 2 tablespoons of the oil and season well. Place in a large, shallow roasting pan and cook in a preheated oven, at 425°F, for 5 minutes.

- Meanwhile, mix the remaining oil with the mustard and garlic and season to taste. Spread over the skin of the lamb, then sprinkle the rosemary and bread crumbs on top and press lightly into place.

- Arrange the lamb racks in the roasting pan and cook for 20 minutes, until the vegetables are tender and the lamb is cooked to your liking, then remove the lamb and vegetables from the pan and keep warm.

- Place the roasting pan over gentle heat on the stove and add the balsamic vinegar, red currant jelly, and stock. Let simmer for 2 minutes, then serve with the meat and vegetables.

 Broiled Lamb and Rosemary Skewers

Mix together the finely grated rind of 1 lemon, 1 teaspoon chopped rosemary, and 1 tablespoon olive oil. Rub over 12 oz lamb cubes, then thread onto metal skewers. Season to taste and cook under a preheated hot broiler for 5–7 minutes, turning often, until golden and cooked through. Serve in toasted baguettes with red currant jelly and a large handful of mixed salad greens.

 Greek Roasted Lamb with Rosemary Place 4 thick lamb cutlets in a roasting pan with 2 small halved tomatoes and 2 cored, seeded, and sliced red bell peppers. Drizzle with 1 tablespoon olive oil, sprinkle with 2 teaspoons chopped oregano and 1 teaspoon chopped rosemary, and season well. Place in a preheated oven, at 400°F, for 15 minutes, until the lamb is cooked through. Stir in 1 (15 oz) can lima beans, rinsed and drained. Serve sprinkled with chopped parsley and ⅓ cup crumbled feta cheese.

ONE-MEAT-BIF

20 Italian Hamburgers with Polenta Fries

Serves 4

1 shallot, finely chopped
1 egg yolk
1 lb ground beef
¼ cup olive oil
1 lb Italian-style polenta log, cut into sticks
4 oz mozzarella cheese, sliced
4 tomatoes, chopped
2 teaspoons balsamic vinegar
handful of chopped basil
4 ciabatta rolls, lightly toasted
handful of arugula
salt and black pepper

- Mix together three-quarters of the shallot, the egg yolk, and beef and season well. Wet your hands and shape the mixture into 4 patties. Brush all over with a little oil, place on a baking sheet, and cook under a preheated hot broiler for 5 minutes, until golden.

- Turn the burgers over, arrange the polenta fries on the baking sheet, and drizzle with a little more oil. Cook for another 3 minutes, then turn over the polenta fries and place the mozzarella on top of the burgers. Return to the broiler for 1–2 minutes, until the cheese has melted and the polenta fries are golden.

- Meanwhile, mix together the tomatoes, the remaining shallot and oil, the balsamic vinegar, and basil and season to taste. Place the burgers in the buns with a handful of arugula and serve with the tomato salad and polenta fries.

 Italian Grilled Beef Sandwiches

Rub 1 tablespoon olive oil all over 4 top sirloin steaks and season well. Cook in a smoking hot ridged grill pan for 2–3 minutes on each side. Mix 2 tablespoons pesto with ¼ cup mayonnaise and spread on 4 slices of lightly toasted sourdough bread. Cut the steaks into thin strips and arrange on the bread, then chop 2 tomatoes and sprinkle on top with a sprinkling of basil leaves. Serve immediately.

 Italian Stewed Beef

Heat 2 tablespoons olive oil in a large, heavy saucepan over high heat. Add 12 oz top sirloin steak, cut into strips, and cook for 2–3 minutes, until golden, then remove from the pan and set aside. Reduce the heat, add 1 chopped onion to the pan, and cook for 5 minutes, until softened, then stir in 1 cored, seeded, and sliced yellow bell pepper, 2 crushed garlic cloves, 2 teaspoons tomato paste, and a pinch each of dried red pepper flakes and dried oregano. Pour in ½ cup dry white wine and simmer for 3 minutes, then add 1 (14½ oz) can diced tomatoes. Bring to a boil, then reduce the heat and simmer for 15 minutes. Return the beef to the pan and cook for another 3 minutes, until heated through, then serve with ciabatta bread.

ONE-MEAT-CAN

30 Roast Pork with Fennel and Lemon

Serves 4

2 (12 oz) pork tenderloins
2 tablespoons olive oil
2 lemons
1½ lb small new potatoes, halved
1 fennel bulb, sliced
3–4 sage leaves
salt and black pepper

- Rub the pork with a little of the oil and place in a large, shallow roasting pan. Finely grate the rind of 1 lemon and sprinkle with the pork with salt and plenty of pepper.

- Sprinkle the potatoes around the pork and drizzle with the remaining oil. Place in a preheated oven, at 425°F, for 10 minutes.

- Cut the other lemon into wedges and add to the roasting pan with the fennel and sage leaves. Return to the oven for 15 minutes, until the meat and potatoes are cooked through.

 Pork Chops with Fennel and Lemon Coleslaw Rub a pinch of chili powder and 1 tablespoon olive oil over 4 pork chops and season well. Heat a ridged grill pan until smoking hot, then cook the pork for 4 minutes on each side, until golden and cooked through. Meanwhile, finely slice 2 fennel bulbs and mix with ⅓ cup mayonnaise, 1 tablespoon lemon juice, and a handful of chopped parsley. Serve the coleslaw with the chops.

 Fennel and Lemon Porkballs with Cannellini Beans Mix 12 oz ground pork with the finely grated rind of 1 lemon, 1 teaspoon crushed fennel seeds, ½ finely chopped red chile, 1 cup fresh white bread crumbs, and 1 egg yolk. Season to taste and use wet hands to shape into 12 balls. Heat 1 tablespoon olive oil in a flameproof casserole dish. Sauté the balls for 5 minutes, until golden, then add 1 cup hot chicken stock and simmer for 5 minutes. Add 8 halved cherry tomatoes and 1 (15 oz) can cannellini beans, rinsed and drained. Cook for another 5 minutes, until heated through, then serve sprinkled with chopped basil.

ONE-MEAT-WUZ

10 Herbed Pork and Lentil Salad

Serves 4

1 shallot, finely chopped

2 tablespoons extra virgin olive oil

finely grated rind and juice of
½ lemon

handful of chopped parsley

1¼ cups canned lentils, rinsed
and drained, or cooked lentils

1 teaspoon capers, rinsed and
drained

5 oz pulled pork

8 cherry tomatoes, halved

5 cups arugula

- Mix together the shallot, oil, lemon rind and juice, and parsley and then stir the mixture into the lentils.

- Add the capers, pork, tomatoes, and arugula. Season to taste and arrange on a platter to serve.

---

20 Spicy Pork and Lentil Wraps

Heat 1 tablespoon vegetable oil in a large, heavy saucepan. Add 2 crushed garlic cloves, 1 teaspoon ground cumin, 1 teaspoon ground paprika, and ½ teaspoon ground coriander and cook for 30 seconds, then add ¾ cup canned diced tomatoes and ½ cup water, season to taste, and simmer for 10 minutes. Add 2 cups canned lentils, rinsed and drained, or cooked lentils and 3 oz pulled pork and cook for 5 minutes, then stir in a large handful of chopped fresh cilantro. Heat 4 wheat tortillas briefly in an oven or microwave, then spoon the sauce over them and fold up to make packages.

30 Ham and Lentil Soup with Arugula Salsa Verde

Heat 2 tablespoons olive oil in a large, heavy saucepan. Add 1 chopped onion, 1 chopped carrot, and 1 chopped celery stick and cook for 5 minutes, until softened, then add 6 cups hot chicken stock and 8 oz ham steaks, cut into bite-size pieces. Bring to a boil, then reduce the heat and simmer for 10 minutes. Add 2 cups canned lentils, rinsed and drained, or cooked lentils, season to taste, and cook for another 2 minutes, until soft. Meanwhile, place 5 cups arugula in a food processor with 1 crushed garlic clove, 1 teaspoon capers, rinsed and drained, 1 tablespoon lemon juice, and ¼ cup extra virgin olive oil and blend until smooth. Serve the soup drizzled with the salsa verde.

ONE-MEAT-LER

30 Spicy Beef and Squash Stew with Corn

Serves 4

2 tablespoons vegetable oil

2 large top sirloin steaks, cut into chunks

1 onion, finely chopped

1 small butternut squash, peeled and cut into chunks

1 red chile, seeded and chopped

1 teaspoon ground cumin

1 tablespoon tomato paste

1 (14½ oz) can plum tomatoes

1 cup canned corn kernels

handful of chopped fresh cilantro, to garnish

- Heat half the oil in a large, heavy saucepan. Add the steak and cook over high heat for about 3 minutes, until browned, then remove from the pan and set aside.

- Add the remaining oil to the pan with the onion and squash and cook for 5 minutes, until softened. Stir in the chile and cumin and cook for 30 seconds, then add the tomato paste and tomatoes and simmer for 15 minutes.

- Return the beef to the pan with the corn and heat through. Serve sprinkled with the cilantro.

 Seared Beef and Tomatoes with Polenta Heat 2 tablespoons oil in a nonstick skillet. Add 1 lb Italian-style polenta log, thickly sliced, and cook for 1 minute on each side, until golden. Season to taste, remove from the skillet, and keep warm. Add 4 small top sirloin steaks to the skillet and cook for 2 minutes. Turn the steaks over and add 8 halved cherry tomatoes to the skillet. Cook for 2–3 minutes, until the steaks are cooked to your liking. Season to taste, sprinkle with chopped basil, and spoon over the polenta slices to serve.

Beef, Tomato, and Beans with Nacho Topping Heat 1 tablespoon oil in a large, flameproof skillet. Add 1 finely chopped onion and cook for 2 minutes, then stir in 10 oz ground beef. Cook for 5 minutes, until golden, then add 1 teaspoon each of ground coriander and cumin. Stir in ¾ cup canned diced tomatoes and simmer for 10 minutes, topping up with a little water, if necessary. Add 1 cup canned kidney beans, rinsed and drained, and heat through. Arrange 3 oz of tortilla chips on top of the stew and sprinkle with ½ cup shredded cheddar cheese. Cook under a preheated hot broiler for 1–2 minutes, until the cheese melts. Serve with sour cream, guacamole, and salsa.

30 Pork and Paprika Goulash

Serves 4

2 tablespoons vegetable oil
1 lb pork tenderloin, cubed
1 onion, sliced
2 teaspoons smoked paprika
1 (14½ oz) can diced tomatoes
1 lb potatoes, diced
salt and black pepper
¼ cup sour cream
handful of chopped parsley,
  to garnish

- Heat half the oil in a deep skillet. Add the pork, season to taste, and cook for 5 minutes, until browned all over. Remove from the skillet and set aside. Add the remaining oil to the skillet with the onion and cook for 5 minutes, until softened.

- Stir in the paprika, then add the tomatoes and potatoes. Season to taste, bring to a boil, then reduce the heat and simmer for 10 minutes.

- Return the pork to the skillet and cook for another 5 minutes, until the pork and potatoes are cooked through. Divide among serving bowls, top with the sour cream, and serve sprinkled with parsley.

---

10 Chorizo and Roasted Pepper Sandwiches with Paprika

Heat a ridged grill pan until smoking hot, then cook 2 red bell peppers, cored, seeded, and cut into thick wedges, for 3–4 minutes, until blackened. Remove the peppers from the pan and set aside. Add 8 oz cooked chorizo sausage, halved lengthwise, to the pan and cook for 1–2 minutes, until browned. Lightly toast 4 ciabatta rolls and rub the cut surfaces with a peeled garlic clove. Cut the roasted peppers and chorizo into slices and divide among the rolls. Top with a handful of arugula, a little sour cream, and a sprinkling of smoked paprika.

20 Crispy Paprika Pork Chops with Roasted Peppers

Mix ¾ cup dried bread crumbs with the finely grated rind of ½ lemon and 2 teaspoons smoked paprika. Dip 4 pork chops into olive oil, then press into the bread crumb mixture and season to taste. Arrange the chops on a baking sheet with 2 sliced red bell peppers. Place in a preheated oven, at 425°F, for 15 minutes, until the pork is cooked through, then serve with a green salad.

 Sweet Potato and Chorizo Hash

Serves 4

3 tablespoons olive oil
4 oz chorizo, thickly sliced
1 onion, sliced
3 sweet potatoes, peeled
  and diced
¼ cup fresh green pesto
1 tablespoon lemon juice
2 teaspoons capers, rinsed
  and drained
6 cups arugula
salt and black pepper

- Heat 1 tablespoon of the oil in a large nonstick skillet. Add the chorizo and cook for 2 minutes, until golden, then remove from the skillet and set aside.

- Add the onion to the skillet and cook for 3 minutes, until starting to soften, then add the sweet potatoes. Cook gently for another 10 minutes, until the sweet potatoes are tender, then season to taste. Return the chorizo to the skillet and heat through.

- Mix the pesto with the lemon juice and capers. Serve the arugula with the sweet potato hash and drizzle with the pesto.

 Sweet Potato Pasta with Chorizo

Cook 12 oz quick-cook penne pasta in a large saucepan of lightly salted boiling water according to the package directions, adding 2 peeled and diced sweet potatoes for the last 6 minutes of cooking. Drain and return the pasta and sweet potatoes to the pan. Add 3 oz thin chorizo slices, cut into quarters, the finely grated rind and juice of ½ lemon, 3 tablespoons olive oil, and 4 cups arugula. Season to taste and serve immediately.

 Sweet Potato and Chorizo Soup

Heat 1 tablespoon olive oil in a large, heavy saucepan. Add 4 oz diced chorizo and cook for 2 minutes, until golden, then remove from the pan and set aside. Add 1 finely chopped onion to the pan and cook for 5 minutes, until softened, then add 3 chopped sweet potatoes, cover, and cook gently for 10 minutes, until tender. Add 1 crushed garlic clove and a pinch of dried red pepper flakes, then pour in 6 cups vegetable stock. Simmer for 10 minutes, then use a handheld immersion blender to puree the soup until smooth. Stir in ⅓ cup crème fraîche or heavy cream, then ladle the soup into warm serving bowls and sprinkle with the chorizo to serve.

QuickCook
Vegetarian

Recipes listed by cooking time

30

20

10

30 Crispy Spinach and Feta Pie

Serves 4

1 (10 oz) packge frozen spinach
2 scallions, chopped
1 garlic clove, crushed
1⅓ cups crumbled feta cheese
2 eggs, beaten
pinch of grated nutmeg
2 tablespoons butter, melted
3 tablespoons olive oil
5 large phyllo pastry sheets
salt and black pepper

- Place the spinach in a strainer, then pour over boiling water to defrost. Squeeze to remove excess water, then mix with the scallions, garlic, feta, and eggs. Add the nutmeg and season to taste.

- Stir together the butter and oil and brush over the sides and bottom of an 8 inch springform cake pan. Unwrap the phyllo pastry and cover with damp paper towels until ready to use it.

- Working quickly, brush 1 sheet with the butter mixture and arrange in the pan, letting the excess pastry hang over the sides. Brush another sheet with the butter mixture, turn the pan a little, and arrange the pastry in the same way. Repeat the process until the bottom and sides of the pan are completely covered.

- Spoon the filling into the pan, then fold the pastry edges in to cover the filling, scrunching them up a little as you work. Brush the top of the pie with a little more butter mixture and cook in a preheated oven, at 400°F, for 20–25 minutes, until golden and crisp.

 Spinach, Feta, and Chickpea Salad Beat together 1 tablespoon lemon juice, 3 tablespoons olive oil, and a pinch of ground cumin. Toss with 1 (15 oz) can chickpeas, rinsed and drained, and ½ thinly sliced red onion and season well. Stir in 4 cups baby spinach leaves and 1 chopped roasted pepper from a jar, and arrange on a serving plate. Crumble ½ cup feta cheese over the top and serve.

 Spinach Pancakes with Tomato and Feta Salsa Place 1⅔ cups all-purpose flour and 1 tablespoon baking powder in a mixing bowl. Stir in 1 egg, 1¼ cups milk, and a good pinch of salt, then beat until smooth. Add 3 cups finely chopped spinach. Heat a large, nonstick skillet, add 1 tablespoon butter, and swirl around the skillet. Drop heaping tablespoons of the batter into the skillet and cook for 2–3 minutes on each side until puffed and set. Keep warm while you cook the remainder. Meanwhile, mix together 3 chopped tomatoes, 1 cup crumbled feta cheese, a handful of chopped oregano, 2 tablespoons olive oil, and 1 teaspoon red wine vinegar. Season to taste and spoon the mixture over the pancakes to serve.

ONE-VEGE-TOB

Sweet Potato and Coconut Curry

Serves 4

1 tablespoon vegetable oil

1 onion, chopped

2 garlic cloves, crushed

1 tablespoon finely grated fresh ginger root

2 tablespoons Thai red curry paste

1¾ cups coconut milk

1 cup hot vegetable stock

1 teaspoon granulated sugar

1 tablespoon Thai fish sauce

2 lemon grass stalks

3 sweet potatoes, peeled and diced

2 large tomatoes, quartered

salt and black pepper

2 tablespoons lime juice

handful of chopped fresh cilantro

¼ cup bean sprouts

- Heat the oil in a large, heavy saucepan. Add the onion and cook for 3–5 minutes, until softened. Stir in the garlic and ginger, followed by the curry paste, and cook for 1 minute. Add the coconut milk, stock, sugar, fish sauce, and lemon grass and bring to a boil.

- Add the sweet potatoes to the pan and simmer for 10 minutes, until tender, then add the tomatoes and cook for another 2 minutes. Divide the curry among warm bowls, pour the lime juice over it, and top with the cilantro and bean sprouts to serve.

Sweet Potato and Coconut Soup

Heat 1 tablespoon vegetable oil in a large saucepan. Add 1 crushed garlic clove, 2 teaspoons grated ginger root, and 2 teaspoons Thai red curry paste. Cook for 30 seconds, then add 2 finely chopped sweet potatoes. Pour in 1 cup coconut milk and 4 cups hot vegetable stock, bring to a boil, and cook for 7 minutes, until tender. Use a handheld immersion blender to puree the soup until smooth. Sprinkle with chopped cilantro.

Sweet Potato, Coconut, and Lemon Grass Risotto

Heat 1 tablespoon vegetable oil in a deep skillet. Add 1 peeled and finely chopped sweet potato and cook for 5 minutes, until golden. Remove from the skillet and set aside. Add 1 finely chopped onion to the skillet, with a little more oil if necessary, and cook for 5 minutes, until softened. Stir in 2 crushed garlic cloves and 1 teaspoon finely grated fresh ginger root, cook for 30 seconds, then add 1½ cups risotto rice. Stir well, then add 1¼ cups hot vegetable stock, 2 lemon grass stalks, and 2 kaffir lime leaves. Simmer, stirring continuously, until the liquid has been absorbed, then add 1¾ cups coconut milk. When the rice is beginning to dry out again, return the sweet potato to the skillet and add another 1¼ cups stock. Continue to cook, adding more stock if necessary, until the rice is tender. Season to taste and serve sprinkled with chopped fresh cilantro.

30 Tomato and Basil Tart

Serves 4

butter for greasing
1 sheet ready-to-bake
  puff pastry
all-purpose flour, for dusting
1 egg, beaten
1 cup mascarpone cheese
½ cup grated Parmesan cheese
handful of chopped basil, plus
  extra to garnish
10 cherry tomatoes, halved
1 tablespoon olive oil
salt and black pepper

- Lightly grease a baking sheet. Roll out the pastry to a 12 inch circle. Place on the baking sheet and roll the edges up to create a ½ inch border.

- Press the border down with your thumb to make a crumpled edge, then prick over the middle of the pastry circle a few times with a fork. Place in the freezer for a few minutes.

- Brush the border of the pastry with a little of the beaten egg. Mix together the mascarpone, remaining egg, Parmesan, and basil, season to taste, and spread over the center of the tart. Top with the tomatoes and drizzle with the oil.

- Place in a preheated oven, at 425°F, for 20–25 minutes, until golden and crisp.

 Tomato and Basil Omelets

Beat 1 tablespoon fresh green pesto with 4 eggs. Heat 1 teaspoon butter in a small skillet and add one-quarter of the egg mixture. Stir for 10 seconds, then let set. Sprinkle with a little grated Parmesan cheese and 3 halved cherry tomatoes. Fold over and keep warm, then repeat to make 4 omelets in all. Serve with new potatoes and mixed salad greens, if desired.

 Creamy Tomato and Basil Soup

Heat 2 tablespoons olive oil in a large, heavy saucepan. Add 1 finely chopped onion and cook for 5 minutes, until softened. Add 1 (14½ oz) can diced tomatoes and 4 cups hot vegetable stock and bring to a boil, then reduce the heat and simmer for 10 minutes. Stir in a handful of chopped basil, then use a handheld immersion blender to puree the soup until smooth.

Add ⅓ cup heavy cream, season, heat through, and serve with ciabatta rolls, if desired.

30 Zingy Wild Mushroom Rice

Serves 4

2 tablespoons butter

1 tablespoon olive oil

8 oz wild mushrooms, coarsely chopped

1 onion, finely chopped

2 garlic cloves, crushed

1½ cups mixed wild and long grain rice

3 cups vegetable stock

finely grated rind and juice of 1 lemon

2 scallions, chopped

large handful of chopped parsley

½ red chile, chopped

salt and black pepper

- Heat the butter and oil in a large, heavy saucepan. Add the mushrooms and cook for 3 minutes, until golden, then remove from the pan and set aside. Add the onion to the pan and cook for 5 minutes, until softened, then stir in the garlic. Add the rice and stir until coated in the oil, then pour in the stock.

- Bring to a boil, then reduce the heat and simmer for about 15 minutes, until most of the liquid has been absorbed. Return the mushrooms to the pan, cover, and cook very gently for 5–7 minutes, until the rice is tender. Season to taste and stir in the remaining ingredients before serving.

---

10 Thai Mushroom and Rice Noodle Soup

Heat 1 tablespoon vegetable oil in a large saucepan. Add 1 tablespoon Thai red curry paste and cook for 30 seconds. Add 6 cups hot vegetable stock, 1 lemon grass stalk, and 5 oz shiitake mushrooms, halved if large. Simmer for 3 minutes, then add 4 oz rice noodles, cooked. Heat through, divide among serving bowls, and serve topped with a handful of bean sprouts and chopped fresh cilantro.

20 Mushroom and Rice Cakes

Heat 1 tablespoon butter and 1 tablespoon olive oil in a nonstick skillet. Add 1 crushed garlic clove and 2 cups finely chopped mushrooms and cook for 5 minutes. Remove from the skillet and cool. Mix the mushrooms with 1 egg yolk, 2 cups cooked rice, ¼ cup grated Parmesan cheese, the finely grated rind of ½ lemon, a pinch of dried red pepper flakes, and a handful of chopped parsley. Season to taste and shape into small cakes with your hands, then lightly coat with a little flour. Heat a little more oil in the skillet, then cook the cakes for 3 minutes on each side until golden and cooked through. Serve with a tomato salad.

 # Chickpea and Red Pepper Soup

Serves 4

2 tablespoons olive oil
1 onion, finely chopped
1 red bell pepper, cored, seeded, and chopped
2 garlic cloves, crushed
2 teaspoons tomato paste
1 teaspoon ground cumin
½ teaspoon ground coriander
pinch of cayenne pepper
pinch of saffron threads
6 cups hot vegetable stock
1 (15 oz) can chickpeas, rinsed and drained
⅔ cup couscous
finely grated rind and juice of 1 lemon
salt and black pepper
handful of chopped mint
handful of chopped fresh cilantro

- Heat the oil in a large, heavy saucepan. Add the onion and cook for 5 minutes, then add the red bell pepper, garlic, tomato paste, and spices and cook for another 1 minute.

- Pour in the stock and bring to a boil, then reduce the heat and simmer for 5 minutes. Add the chickpeas and simmer for another 5 minutes, then season to taste.

- Add the couscous and a squeeze of lemon juice and cook for 1 minute until the couscous is tender. Divide among serving bowls and sprinkle with the herbs and grated lemon rind before serving.

 ### Chickpea and Red Pepper Couscous

Heat 1 tablespoon olive oil in a large, heavy saucepan. Add 2 sliced garlic cloves and cook for 1 minute, then add 1 roasted pepper from a jar, 1 cup rinsed and drained, canned chickpeas, and 1 cup couscous. Remove from the heat. Pour in 1 cup hot vegetable stock, cover, and let rest for 5 minutes, until tender. Stir in a good squeeze of lemon juice and 4 cups arugula.

 ### Chickpea and Red Pepper Burgers

Place 2 (15 oz) cans chickpeas, rinsed and well drained, in a food processor with 1 crushed garlic clove, the finely grated rind of ½ lemon, a handful of mint leaves, ½ cup dried bread crumbs, and 1 egg yolk, and blend to form a rough paste. Finely chop 1 roasted red pepper from a jar and stir in, then shape the mixture into 4 large patties. Chill in the refrigerator for 15 minutes.

Heat 2 tablespoons olive oil in a nonstick skillet. Add the patties and cook for 3 minutes on each side, until golden. Serve in lightly toasted buns with sliced tomatoes and a handful of cilantro leaves. Add a drizzle of tahini, if desired.

Squash with Stilton Fondue

Serves 4

2 butternut or other small squash
1 tablespoon olive oil
1 cup crème fraîche or
  Greek yogurt
1 tablespoon cornstarch
6 oz Stilton or other blue cheese,
  rind removed
handful of thyme leaves
salt and black pepper

- Cut the squash in half and trim a thin slice off the rounded back of each half so they will stand securely, cut sides up. Scoop out and discard the seeds and fibers, then score the cut surface of the squash in a crisscross pattern. Drizzle with the oil and season to taste. Arrange on a baking sheet and cook in a preheated oven, at 450°F, for 15 minutes, until tender.

- Meanwhile, mix together the crème fraîche and cornstarch, then mash in the Stilton with a fork and add plenty of black pepper. Divide the mixture among the cavities of the squash halves, sprinkle with the thyme leaves, and return to the oven for another 10 minutes, until the filling is golden and bubbling.

Squash, Stilton, and Spinach Pasta

Cook 1 small butternut squash, peeled and diced, and 12 oz spaghetti in a large saucepan of lightly salted boiling water for 9 minutes or according to the package directions. Add 4 cups baby spinach leaves and drain immediately, then return the spaghetti and vegetables to the pan. Stir in ⅓ cup crème fraîche or heavy and ⅓ cup crumbled Stilton or other blue cheese, season to taste, and serve.

Squash and Stilton Frittata

Heat ¼ cup olive oil in a large nonstick skillet. Add 1 sliced red onion and 1 small butternut squash, peeled and diced, and cook for 5 minutes, until softened. Beat 5 eggs with 2 finely chopped sage leaves and season well. Reduce the heat to low, then pour the eggs into the pan. Crumble ⅓ cup Stilton or other blue cheese over the top, and cook gently for 10–15 minutes, until the eggs are just set.

Corn, Coconut, and Tomato Curry

Serves 4

1 tablespoon vegetable oil
1 onion, finely chopped
2 garlic cloves, finely chopped
1 tablespoon grated fresh
   ginger root
1 teaspoon mustard seeds
1 teaspoon cumin seeds
1 teaspoon ground coriander
½ teaspoon ground turmeric
1 (14½ oz) can diced tomatoes
1 cup coconut milk
4 corn cobs, cut into thick slices
salt and black pepper
handful of chopped fresh cilantro,
   to garnish

- Heat the oil in a large, flameproof casserole dish. Add the onion and cook for 5 minutes, until softened. Stir in the garlic, ginger, and whole spices and cook for 1 minute, until the spices start to sizzle.

- Add the ground spices, stir well, then add the tomatoes and coconut milk. Bring to a boil, then reduce the heat and simmer for 10 minutes.

- Season to taste, add the corn, and cook for 2–3 minutes, until just tender. Serve sprinkled with the cilantro.

 Corn and Coconut Soup

Place 1 small crushed garlic clove in a heavy saucepan with 2 chopped scallions, 1 cup canned corn kernels, 1 chopped red chile, 1 cup coconut milk, and 4 cups hot vegetable stock. Bring to a boil, reduce the heat, and simmer for 8 minutes. Use a handheld immersion blender to puree the soup until smooth. Drizzle with 2 tablespoons lime juice and sprinkle with fresh cilantro leaves to serve.

 Baked Creamy Corn and Coconut

Pour 1¾ cups coconut milk into an ovenproof skillet, add ⅓ cup cornmeal, 1 cup canned corn kernels, and 2 tablespoons butter, and season to taste. Simmer gently for 5 minutes, until starting to thicken, then set aside to cool for 5 minutes. Meanwhile, beat 4 egg whites until stiff peaks form. Beat the 4 egg yolks into the corn mixture, one at a time, then gently fold in the egg whites until well combined. Place in a preheated oven, at 425°F, for 15–20 minutes, until risen and golden. Serve immediately.

 # Pea and Asparagus Risotto

Serves 4

1 tablespoon olive oil
1 onion, finely chopped
1 garlic clove, crushed
1½ cup risotto rice
½ cup dry white wine
4 cups hot vegetable stock
4 oz fine asparagus spears, halved
½ cup frozen peas
2 tablespoons butter
salt and black pepper
3 cups arugula
Parmesan cheese shavings

- Heat the oil in a large, heavy saucepan. Add the onion and cook for 5 minutes, until softened. Add the garlic and rice and cook for 30 seconds, until coated in the oil. Pour in the wine and simmer until boiled away.

- Gradually add the stock, a ladleful at a time, stirring continuously and allowing each ladleful to be absorbed before adding the next. After 10 minutes, add the asparagus, then cook for another 5 minutes, until the rice is tender.

- Stir in the peas and butter, cover, and let stand for 1–2 minutes. Season the risotto taste, then spoon into warm bowls and top each serving with a handful of arugula and some Parmesan shavings.

 Pea and Mushroom Fried Rice

Heat 1 tablespoon vegetable oil in a deep skillet. Add 5 oz halved shiitake mushrooms and cook for 2 minutes, until softened. Add 2 sliced scallions, 2 cups snow peas, 1 crushed garlic clove, and 1 teaspoon grated fresh ginger root. Cook for 1 minute, then add 2 cups cooked rice and ½ cup frozen peas. Cook for 2 minutes, then push the mixture to the sides of the skillet. Crack an egg into the center and stir to scramble.

When set, stir the egg into the rice with 2–3 tablespoons soy sauce and serve immediately.

Pea, Asparagus, and Rice Soup

Heat 2 tablespoons olive oil in a large, heavy saucepan. Add 1 chopped onion and 1 chopped leek and cook for 5 minutes, until softened. Pour in 5 cups hot vegetable stock and simmer for 5 minutes. Add 5 oz asparagus tips and cook for 2 minutes, then add ½ cup fozen peas and ⅔ cup cooked rice. Season to taste. Heat through, ladle into bowls, and serve sprinkled with chopped parsley and grated Parmesan cheese.

ONE-VEGE-XOI

10 Fried Cheese and Zucchini with Red Pepper Salsa

Serves 4

2 tablespoons olive oil

8 oz baby zucchini, halved lengthwise

8 oz Muenster or mozzarella cheese, thickly sliced

salt and black pepper

For the salsa

2 roasted red peppers from a jar, finely chopped

1 garlic clove, crushed

1 red chile, seeded and finely chopped

finely grated rind and juice of ½ lemon

2 tablespoons extra virgin olive oil

handful of chopped mint

- Heat half the olive oil in a large skillet. Add the zucchini and cook for 2 minutes, then turn over and cook for another 1 minute, until golden. Season to taste, remove from the skillet, and keep warm.

- Add the remaining olive oil to the skillet, followed by the cheese. Cook for 1–2 minutes on each side, until golden.

- Meanwhile, mix together all the ingredients for the salsa. Divide the zucchini and cheese among serving plates and spoon the salsa over them to serve.

 Cheese, Zucchini, and Red Pepper Kebabs Cut 8 oz Muenster or mozzarella cheese, 2 large zucchini, and 2 red bell peppers into large chunks. Toss with 2 tablespoons olive oil, season to taste, and thread onto metal skewers. Heat a ridged grill pan until smoking hot. Split 4 pita breads in half horizontally, then cut into strips. Drizzle 2 tablespoons olive oil over the pita strips and cook in the grill pan for 1 minute, until browned and lightly crisp. Remove from the pan and keep warm, then cook the kebabs in the pan for 3–5 minutes, turning occasionally, until golden. Meanwhile, toss 1 (15 oz) can chickpeas, rinsed and drained, with 1 small sliced red onion and a large handful of chopped basil and parsley. Drizzle with oil, season to taste, and serve with the kebabs and pita strips.

Roasted Cheese and Zucchini-Stuffed Peppers Cut 4 red or yellow bell peppers in half lengthwise, remove the seeds, and place on a baking sheet, cut sides up. Drizzle with 1 tablespoon olive oil and season well. Place in a preheated oven, at 400°F, for 10 minutes. Coarsely grate 2 small zucchini and mix with 1 beaten egg and 1 cup ricotta cheese. Season and spoon into the bell peppers. Top the filling with a slice of mozzarella cheese and return to the oven for 10–15 minutes, until golden and just set.

30 Beet Risotto with Goat Cheese

Serves 4

1 tablespoon vegetable oil
1 onion, finely chopped
1 garlic clove, finely chopped
1¼ cups risotto rice
⅔ cup dry white wine
3½ cups hot vegetable stock
3 cups diced cooked beets
  (not in vinegar)
2 tablespoons butter
4 oz goat cheese
salt and black pepper
handful of chopped dill, to garnish

- Heat the oil in a large, heavy saucepan. Add the onion and cook for 5 minutes, until softened. Add the garlic and rice and cook for 30 seconds, until coated in the oil. Pour in the wine and simmer until boiled away.

- Gradually add the stock, a ladleful at a time, stirring continuously and allowing each ladleful to be absorbed before adding the next. This should take about 15 minutes.

- Meanwhile, place half the beet in a food processor with a little of the stock and blend to a smooth puree.

- When the rice is nearly ready, add the diced and pureed beet. Cook for 2–3 minutes, until the rice is tender, then stir in the butter, cover, and let stand for 1 minute. Season to taste, then spoon into warm bowls and serve sprinkled with the goat cheese and dill.

---

10 Beet and Broiled Goat Cheese Salad

Cut 3 oz of a goat cheese log into thick slices. Place on a greased baking sheet and cook under a preheated hot broiler for 3 minutes, until just golden and melted. Beat 1 tablespoon sherry vinegar with 1 tablespoon finely chopped shallot and 3 tablespoons extra virgin olive oil. Season, then toss with 2 cups diced cooked beet and 1 (5 oz) package mixed salad greens. Divide among serving plates, then place the goat cheese on top and sprinkle with ¼ cup coarsely chopped walnuts.

20 Beet and Goat Cheese Stacks

Cut 8 oz cooked beet into thin slices. Mix ⅓ cup crème fraîche or Greek yogurt with 8 oz soft goat cheese until smooth. Lightly grease four 3 inch metal molds or large individual ramekins and place a slice of beet in the bottom of each. Spread a layer of the goat cheese mixture on top, then add another slice of beet. Repeat the layers to use up the remaining ingredients. Place in a preheated oven, at 350°F, for 15–20 minutes, until heated through. Turn

out onto plates and serve with a green salad.

 **Feta-Stuffed Roasted Peppers**

Serves 4

1 tablespoon olive oil
4 long sweet peppers
2 egg yolks
1⅓ cups crumbled feta cheese
3 tablespoons plain yogurt
finely grated rind of ½ lemon
1 teaspoon chopped oregano

- Rub the oil over the sweet peppers, arrange them in a broiler pan, and cook under a preheated hot broiler for 5 minutes, turning once, until just soft. Let cool for a couple of minutes, then cut in half lengthwise and remove the seeds.

- Place the egg yolks, three-quarters of the feta, the yogurt, and lemon rind in a food processor and blend until smooth. Spoon the mixture into the sweet peppers, then crumble the remaining feta on top and sprinkle with the oregano.

- Return to the broiler and cook for 5–7 minutes, until golden and cooked through. Let set for a couple of minutes before serving.

 Feta and Roasted Pepper Salad

Mash ⅔ cup feta cheese with 2 tablespoons heavy cream until well combined and smooth. Spoon the mixture into 4 roasted pepper halves from a jar and roll up. Beat 1 tablespoon lemon juice with 3 tablespoons olive oil and ½ teaspoon dried oregano, then season to taste. Toss together with 3½ cups mache or other salad greens, ½ sliced cucumber, and ½ cup pitted ripe black olives. Arrange the salad on a serving platter, cut the roasted peppers into thick slices, and arrange on top. Serve with crusty bread.

 Spicy Baked Feta with Roasted Peppers

Lightly grease 4 large sheets of aluminum foil. Divide 1 thinly sliced red onion among the sheets and top with 2 chopped roasted peppers from a jar and a handful of halved cherry tomatoes. Place a 4 oz chunk of feta cheese on top of each serving and divide a handful of chopped oregano and 1 sliced red chile among them. Drizzle with a little olive oil, then fold up the foil to make airtight packages. Place on a baking sheet and cook in a preheated oven, at 400°F, for 20 minutes. Serve with plenty of crusty bread.

 # Thai Mixed Vegetable Soup

Serves 4

1 tablespoon vegetable oil
1 tablespoon Thai red curry paste
pinch of ground turmeric
2/3 cup coconut milk
4 cups hot vegetable stock
1 lemon grass stalk
8 baby corn
4 oz shiitake mushrooms, halved
4 oz rice noodles, cooked
2 cups sugar snap peas
1/2 cup bean sprouts
handful of chopped fresh cilantro
lime wedges, to serve

- Heat the oil in a large, heavy saucepan. Add the curry paste and turmeric and cook for 1 minute, then stir in the coconut milk, stock, and lemon grass and simmer for 2 minutes.

- Add the baby corn and mushrooms and cook for 2 minutes, then add the noodles and sugar snap peas and cook for another 3 minutes. Ladle into warm serving bowls and top with the bean sprouts. Sprinkle with the cilantro leaves and serve with lime wedges.

 ### Thai Mixed Vegetable Stir-Fry

Slice 4 oz tofu and pat dry with paper towels. Heat 2 tablespoons oil in a wok or large skillet. Add the tofu and stir-fry for 3 minutes, until golden all over, then remove from the work and set aside. Add more oil if necessary, then stir-fry 1 sliced onion for 2–3 minutes, until softened. Stir in 1 teaspoon Thai red curry paste, 2 crushed garlic cloves, and 2 teaspoons finely grated fresh ginger root. Stir for 1 minute, then add 1 cored, seeded, and sliced red bell pepper, 2 cups snow peas, and 8 baby corn. Stir-fry for 3–4 minutes, until tender, then return the tofu to the wok with 4 oz rice noodles, cooked, and 1/2 cup bean sprouts. Pour in 2 tablespoons soy sauce and 1 tablespoon sweet chili sauce and cook until the noodles have heated through, adding a little water if necessary. Serve with lime wedges.

Thai Mixed Vegetable Rice

Cook 1 finely chopped onion in 1 tablespoon oil for 5 minutes, then stir in 2 chopped garlic cloves and 1 tablespoon grated ginger root. Cook for 30 seconds, then stir in 1 tablespoon Thai red curry paste. Add 1 1/2 cups basmati or long grain rice, 1 sliced red bell pepper, and 1/2 diced butternut squash. Cook for 1 minute, then pour in 3 cups hot vegetable stock and 1 cup coconut milk. Cook for 10–12 minutes, until most of the liquid is gone, then cover and cook over low heat for 5 minutes, until the rice is cooked through. Sprinkle with cilantro.

30 Red Pepper and Goat Cheese Lasagne

Serves 4

butter, for greasing
2 roasted red peppers from a jar, chopped
handful of chopped basil
2 cups tomato sauce
4 oz soft, rindless goat cheese
⅔ cup mascarpone cheese
⅓ cup milk
8 fresh lasagna noodles
⅓ cup ricotta cheese
¼ cup grated Parmesan cheese
salt and black pepper

- Lightly grease an ovenproof dish. Stir the roasted red peppers and basil into the tomato sauce. Mix together the goat cheese, mascarpone, and milk and season to taste.

- Pour one-quarter of the tomato sauce in the ovenproof dish, then top with one-third of the goat cheese mixture. Arrange a layer of pasta noodles on top. Repeat the layers until you have 3 layers of pasta, then spread the remaining tomato sauce on top.

- Spoon the ricotta over the sauce and sprinkle with the Parmesan. Place in a preheated oven, at 400°F, for 20–25 minutes, until the pasta is tender.

 Spaghetti with Red Peppers and Goat Cheese Cook 1 lb quick-cook spaghetti in a large saucepan of lightly salted boiling water according to the package directions. Meanwhile, mix 2 chopped roasted red peppers from a jar with 4 oz soft goat cheese, ¼ cup mascarpone cheese, and a good handful of chopped parsley. Drain the pasta, return to the pan, and stir in the sauce. Season to taste and serve sprinkled with toasted slivered almonds and chopped basil.

 Red Pepper Minestrone with Goat Cheese Toasts Heat 2 tablespoons olive oil in a large, heavy saucepan. Add 1 finely chopped onion and cook for 5 minutes, until softened, then stir in 2 cored, seeded, and chopped red bell peppers and 2 sliced garlic cloves. Cook for 1–2 minutes, then add 6 cups hot vegetable stock and bring to a boil. Add 4 oz soup pasta shapes and cook for 5 minutes or according to the package directions. Slice a small baguette, toast the slices, and spread with 3 oz soft goat cheese. Ladle the soup into warm bowls, drizzle with ¼ cup fresh green pesto, and serve with the toasts.

20 Spicy Paneer with Tomatoes, Peas, and Beans

Serves 4

2 tablespoons vegetable oil
8 oz paneer, diced (available from Indian grocery stores)
1 onion, finely chopped
2 garlic cloves, chopped
2 teaspoons finely grated fresh ginger root
1 teaspoon ground coriander
1 teaspoon paprika
1 teaspoon tomato paste
½ cup hot vegetable stock
1½ cup green beans
1 cup frozen peas
1 large chopped tomato
1 teaspoon garam masala
salt and black pepper
Indian-style bread, to serve

- Heat half the oil in a large skillet. Add the paneer, season well, and cook for 3–4 minutes, until golden all over. Remove from the skillet and set aside. Add the remaining oil to the skillet with the onion. Cook for 5 minutes, until softened, then add the garlic and ginger and cook for another 1 minute. Add the spices and cook for 30 seconds.

- Stir in the tomato paste and stock and return the paneer to the pan with the beans. Season to taste, cover, and simmer for 5 minutes. Add the peas and tomatoes and cook for another 3 minutes, then stir in the garam masala. Divide among warm bowls and serve with Indian-style bread.

---

10 Spicy Paneer and Tomato Skewers

Cut 8 oz paneer into large cubes. Mix 1 teaspoon garam masala with ½ teaspoon cumin, a pinch of ground turmeric, a handful of chopped fresh cilantro, and 2 tablespoons vegetable oil. Toss with the paneer, then thread onto metal skewers with some whole cherry tomatoes. Season to taste. Heat a ridged grill pan until smoking hot, then cook the skewers for 3–5 minutes, turning once, until lightly browned. Serve with green salad and Indian-style bread.

30 Spicy Paneer-Topped Peppers with Spinach and Peas

Place 1 (10 oz) package frozen chopped spinach in a strainer and pour over boiling water until wilted, then squeeze thoroughly to remove excess water. Mix with ½ cup frozen peas, 1 teaspoon each of ground cumin and ground coriander, and ¼ cup heavy cream and season to taste. Cut 2 red bell peppers in half lengthwise and remove the seeds. Arrange on a lightly greased baking sheet and spoon the spinach mixture into the cavities. Slice 8 oz paneer and arrange on top. Season well and drizzle with a little oil. Place in a preheated oven, at 400°F, for 20 minutes, until bubbling. Finish off under the broiler if the paneer is not browned.

20 Veggie Bean Chili

Serves 4

2 tablespoons vegetable oil

1 onion, finely chopped

1 red bell pepper, cored, seeded, and sliced

1 garlic clove, crushed

1 teaspoon ground cumin

1 teaspoon chipotle paste or a pinch of chili powder

1 teaspoon dried oregano

½ teaspoon ground coriander

1 (14½ oz) can diced tomatoes

1 (15 oz) can black beans, rinsed and drained

1 cup drained canned corn

salt and black pepper

handful of chopped fresh cilantro,

shredded cheddar cheese

sour cream

tortilla chips, to serve

- Heat the oil in a large, flameproof casserole dish. Add the onion and cook for 5 minutes, until softened, then add the red bell pepper, garlic, spices, and herbs and cook for 30 seconds. Pour in the tomatoes and season to taste. Bring to a boil, then reduce the heat and simmer for 10 minutes.

- Add the beans and corn to the pan and cook for another 3–4 minutes, until heated through. Divide among warm bowls and top each serving with a spoonful of sour cream. Sprinkle with the chopped cilantro and grated cheese, then serve with tortilla chips.

---

10 Chili Bean Tostadas

Cook 4 corn tortillas under a preheated hot broiler for 2 minutes, until crisp. Mix 1 (15 oz) can refried beans with 2 chopped tomatoes and a pinch of dried red pepper flakes and spread over the tortillas. Sprinkle ¾ cup shredded cheddar cheese over the top and return to the broiler for 3 minutes, until the cheese melts. Serve topped with 1 sliced avocado and chopped cilantro.

30 Chili Bean Empanadas

Mix 1 cup canned black beans, rinsed and drained, with ½ cup canned corn kernels, 2 finely chopped scallions, 1 chopped tomato, ½ teaspoon ground cumin, a pinch of dried red pepper flakes, and ¾ cup shredded cheddar cheese. Roll out 1 sheet ready-to-bake puff pastry on a lightly floured surface and cut out 4 circles, 6 inches across. Arrange on a lightly greased baking sheet and divide the bean mixture among them, then brush around the edges with beaten egg. Fold the circles in half to enclose the filling and use your fingers to crimp together the pastry to seal. Brush more egg over the packages and cook in a preheated oven at 400°F, for 20 minutes, until puffed and golden.

ONE-VEGE-WYO

10 Pizza Fiorentina

Serves 4

4 cups baby spinach leaves

4 large wheat tortillas or flatbreads

⅔ cup store-bought tomato sauce

4 oz mozzarella cheese, sliced

4 eggs

¼ cup grated Parmesan cheese

- Place the spinach in a strainer and pour over boiling water until wilted, then squeeze thoroughly to remove excess water.

- Arrange the tortillas on 4 pizza pans. Divide the tomato sauce among them, then sprinkle with the spinach. Arrange the mozzarella on top, then crack an egg in the center of each tortilla.

- Sprinkle the Parmesan over the pizzas, then place in a preheated oven, at 425°F, for 5–7 minutes, until the egg whites are just set.

---

2 **Warm Tomato, Spinach, and Tortilla Salad** Cut 2 large tortillas or flatbreads into wedges. Brush with 1 tablespoon olive oil and place on a lightly greased baking sheet. Cook in a preheated oven, at 400°F, for 5 minutes, until golden and crisp. Set aside and add 1⅓ cups cherry tomatoes to the baking sheet. Drizzle with a little more oil, season to taste, and cook in the oven for 10 minutes, until tender and lightly browned. Beat 1 tablespoon balsamic vinegar with 3 tablespoons extra virgin olive oil and season to taste. Toss with 1 (5 oz) package baby spinach leaves and divide among serving plates. Top with the tomatoes and tortilla wedges, then crumble 3 oz soft goat cheese over the salads to serve.

3 **Tomato, Spinach, and Tortilla Casserole** Place 1 (12 oz) package baby spinach leaves in a strainer and pour over boiling water until wilted, then squeeze thoroughly to remove excess water. Mix with 1 cup ricotta cheese and ½ cup crumbled feta cheese. Divide among 8 small tortillas or flatbreads, roll up to enclose the filling, and place in a lightly greased ovenproof dish, seam side down. Pour 2 cups store-bought tomato sauce over the tortillas and sprinkle with 4 oz sliced mozzarella cheese and ½ cup shredded cheddar cheese. Cook in a preheated oven, at 375°F, for 20 minutes, until bubbling and golden.

ONE-VEGE-VAB

3⓪ Cauliflower with Leeks and Cheese Sauce

Serves 4

1 cauliflower, cut into florets
1 large leek, sliced
2 cups hot vegetable stock
2 tablespoons cornstarch
⅔ cup crème fraîche or heavy cream
1 cup shredded cheddar cheese
salt and black pepper
crusty bread, to serve

- Place the cauliflower and leek in a shallow, flameproof casserole dish and pour in the stock. Cover and simmer for 5 minutes, then pour away half the stock.

- Transfer 3 tablespoons of the remaining stock to a cup and mix in the cornstarch until smooth. Stir in the crème fraîche or heavy cream, then stir the mixture into the dish along with half the cheese. Cook for 1 minute, then season to taste.

- Sprinkle the remaining cheese over the vegetables and place in a preheated oven, at 400°F, for 15–20 minutes, until golden and bubbling. Serve with crusty bread.

 Cauliflower and Blue Cheese Pasta

Cook 1 cauliflower, cut into florets, in a large saucepan of lightly salted boiling water for 8 minutes, then add 1 lb fresh penne pasta and cook according to the package directions. Drain and return the cauliflower and pasta to the pan. Add ½ cup crème fraîche or heavy cream and ½ cup crumbled blue cheese. Stir until the cheese has melted, then serve immediately.

 Cauliflower Cheese Soup

Heat 2 tablespoons butter in a large, heavy saucepan. Add 1 chopped onion and cook for 5 minutes, until softened. Add 1 cauliflower, broken into florets, 4 cups hot vegetable stock, and 1 finely chopped sage leaf. Bring to a boil, reduce the heat, and simmer for 10 minutes, until the cauliflower is tender. Stir in ⅓ cup crème fraîche or heavy cream then use a handheld immersion blender to puree the soup until smooth. Stir in ½ cup shredded cheddar cheese and serve with crusty bread.

ONE-VEGE-JOD

3⓿ Pastry-Topped Summer Vegetables

Serves 4

5 tablespoons olive oil

2 zucchini, finely chopped

1 eggplant, finely chopped

1 red bell pepper, cored, seeded, and thinly sliced

1 sheet ready-to-bake puff pastry

1 egg yolk

1¼ cups store-bought tomato sauce

handful of basil leaves

¼ cup pitted ripe black olives

salt and black pepper

- Place the oil in a shallow ovenproof dish. Add the vegetables, toss to coat, and season well. Place in a preheated oven, at 425°F, for 10 minutes, turning once, until golden.

- Meanwhile, cut the pastry into 4 rectangles and brush with the egg yolk. Stir the tomato sauce, basil, and olives into the vegetables, then place a double layer of wax paper on top.

- Place the pastry on top of the wax paper and return the dish to the oven for 15 minutes, until the pastry is golden and crisp. Slide the pastry off the paper and onto the vegetables and serve immediately.

 Grilled Summer Vegetable Bruschetta Toss 1 thinly sliced zucchini and 2 cored, seeded, and sliced red bell peppers with 3 tablespoons olive oil. Cook in a smoking hot ridged grill pan for 3–5 minutes, turning once, until lightly browned. Season to taste and set aside to cool a little. Slice 1 baguette, toast the slices, and rub with 1 peeled garlic clove. Mix ½ cup ricotta cheese with a large handful of chopped basil and spoon the cheese over the toast. Arrange the vegetables on top, sprinkle with Parmesan shavings, and serve immediately.

 Summer Vegetable Tart Place a sheet of ready-to-bake puff pastry on a lightly greased baking sheet. Score around the edges with a knife to make a ½ inch border, then prick all over the center with a fork. Arrange 3 chopped roasted peppers from a jar, 4 oz of chopped roasted eggplant, and 1 thinly sliced zucchini on top. Sprinkle with 5 oz sliced mozzarella cheese and ¼ cup grated Parmesan cheese. Place in a preheated oven, at 425°F, for 15–17 minutes, until golden and puffed. Drizzle with green pesto and serve with a arugula salad.

 # Tomato and Eggplant Pilaf

Serves 4

¼ cup olive oil

1 eggplant, diced

1 onion, finely chopped

1 tablespoon tomato paste

2 cups bulgur wheat,
   rinsed and drained

1¾ cups hot vegetable stock

1 (14½ oz) can diced tomatoes

pinch of brown sugar

salt and black pepper

plain yogurt, to serve

For the pesto

½ cup toasted walnut pieces

1 garlic clove, crushed

bunch of parsley, chopped

¼ cup extra virgin olive oil

1 tablespoon capers,
   rinsed and drained

- Heat 3 tablespoons of the olive oil in a large, flameproof casserole dish. Add the eggplant and cook for 2–3 minutes, until golden, then season to taste. Add the remaining oil to the dish along with the onion. Cook for 5 minutes, until softened, then stir in the tomato paste.

- Add the bulgur wheat, stock, tomatoes, and sugar. Bring to a boil, then cover the dish, reduce the heat, and simmer gently for 15 minutes, until the bulgur has absorbed all the liquid. Season to taste.

- Meanwhile, make the pesto. Place the walnuts in a food processor with the garlic, parsley, and extra virgin olive oil. Blend to a smooth puree, then stir in the capers and season to taste. Divide the pilaf among serving plates and drizzle with the yogurt and pesto.

 Tomato and Eggplant Bruschetta Place 2 roasted eggplants from a jar in a food processor with ⅓ cup plain yogurt, 1 crushed garlic clove, and a handful of basil. Blend to form a smooth puree and season to taste. Thickly slice 1 baguette, lightly toast the slices, and spoon the eggplant mixture on top. Sprinkle 2 chopped tomatoes and a few leaves of arugula over the bruschetta and serve immediately.

 Baked Tomato, Eggplant, and Mozzarella Slice 4 eggplants lengthwise into long, thick slices, arrange in a lightly greased roasting pan, and season well. Drizzle with 3 tablespoons olive oil, then place in a preheated oven, at 425°F, for 10 minutes. Turn the slices over and return to the oven for another 5 minutes, until golden. Pour 1 cup tomato puree or tomato sauce over the eggplants and sprinkle with 1 cup chopped mozzarella cheese. Season to taste and cook for another 10 minutes, until bubbling and heated through. Sprinkle with basil leaves and serve with crusty bread and a green salad.

30 Baked Mushrooms with Goat Cheese and Arugula

Serves 4

1 lb new potatoes, halved
3 tablespoons olive oil
7 oz portobello mushrooms
2 tablespoons chopped thyme
6 garlic cloves, unpeeled
2 oz soft goat cheese
8 cherry tomatoes
3 tablespoons toasted pine nuts
4 cups arugula
salt and black pepper

- Toss the potatoes with 2 tablespoons olive oil and place in a large, shallow roasting pan. Place in a preheated oven, at 425°F, for 15 minutes, turning once.

- Add the mushrooms, stem side up, thyme, and garlic to the pan, drizzle with the remaining oil, and season well. Place a little goat cheese on each mushroom and return to the oven for another 5 minutes.

- Add the cherry tomatoes and return to the oven for another 5 minutes, until the potatoes and mushrooms are cooked through. Sprinkle with the pine nuts and serve with the arugula.

---

10 Mushroom, Goat Cheese, and Arugula Omelets Heat a little butter in a skillet. Add 2½ cups sliced mushrooms and cook for 2 minutes, then add 1 crushed garlic clove and cook for another 1 minute, until tender. Remove from the skillet and set aside. Beat 5 eggs with 1 cup finely chopped arugula and season to taste. Melt a little more butter in the skillet, add one-quarter of the egg mixture, swirl around, and cook for 1 minute, until just set. Sprinkle with one-quarter of the mushrooms and a little goat cheese, then roll up and keep warm. Repeat with the remaining ingredients to make 4 omelets in all, then serve with crusty bread.

20 Mushroom Burgers with Goat Cheese and Arugula Place 4 large portobello mushrooms on a lightly greased baking sheet. Season well, then place in a preheated oven, at 425°F, for 15 minutes or until tender. Split and lightly toast 4 ciabatta rolls. Place a mushroom on the bottom half of each roll, then divide 2 oz soft goat cheese, ¼ cup fresh green pesto, and 1 thinly sliced tomato among them. Replace the tops and serve with a arugula salad.

3⓪ Wintery Minestrone with Pasta and Beans

Serves 4

2 tablespoons olive oil
1 onion, chopped
1 celery stick, chopped
1 carrot, chopped
1 garlic clove, crushed
1 (14½ oz) can diced tomatoes
6 cups vegetable stock
1 rosemary sprig
5 oz small soup pasta shapes
¼ small head Tuscan kale,
  black-leaf kale, or other
  cabbage (about 4 oz)
1 cup canned cannellini beans,
  rinsed and drained
¼ cup fresh green pesto
¼ cup grated Parmesan cheese
salt and black pepper
crusty bread, to serve

- Heat the oil in a large, heavy saucepan. Add the onion, celery, and carrot and cook for 5 minutes, until softened, then add the garlic and cook for another 1 minute. Pour in the tomatoes and stock, add the rosemary, and bring to a boil. Reduce the heat and simmer for 15 minutes.

- Add the pasta and cabbage and cook for 5–7 minutes, or according to the package directions. Stir in the beans and heat through, then season to taste. Ladle the soup into warm bowls, drizzle with the pesto, sprinkle with the Parmesan, and serve with crusty bread.

 Pasta and Bean Salad

Cook 10 oz orzo pasta in a large saucepan of lightly salted boiling water for 5 minutes. Drain, cool under cold running water, and drain again. Toss with 1 cup canned cannellini beans, rinsed and drained, 10 halved cherry tomatoes, and 1 (5 oz) package arugula. Stir in ¼ cup extra virgin olive oil and 1 tablespoon white wine vinegar, season to taste, and serve sprinkled with grated Parmesan.

 Spring Vegetable Minestrone with Beans Heat 1 tablespoon olive oil in a large, heavy saucepan. Add 1 chopped onion and cook for 5 minutes, until softened. Stir in 1 crushed garlic clove and cook for 30 seconds. Pour in 6 cups hot vegetable stock and the rind of ½ lemon, pared in wide strips, and simmer for 5 minutes. Remove the strips of lemon rind and add 1 cup canned cannellini beans, rinsed and drained, 1 finely chopped zucchini, and 1 cup peas or green beans. Simmer for 3–5 minutes, until the vegetables are just tender, then stir in a handful of chopped basil and serve with crusty bread.

ONE-VEGE-TYM

30 Baked Zucchini and Ricotta

Serves 4

butter, for greasing
2 zucchini
2 cups fresh white bread crumbs
1 cup ricotta cheese
1 cup grated Parmesan cheese
2 eggs, beaten
1 garlic clove, crushed
handful of chopped basil
salt and black pepper

- Lightly grease 8 cups in a large muffin pan. Use a vegetable peeler to make 16 long ribbons of zucchini and set aside. Coarsely shred the remainder of the zucchini and squeeze to remove any excess moisture.

- Mix the shredded zucchini with the remaining ingredients and season well. Arrange 2 zucchini ribbons in a cross shape in each hole of the muffin pan. Spoon in the filling and fold over the overhanging zucchini ends.

- Place in a preheated oven, at 375°F, for 15–20 minutes, or until golden and cooked through. Turn out onto serving plates.

 Penne with Zucchini and Ricotta Cook 1 lb fresh penne pasta in a large saucepan of lightly salted boiling water according to the package directions, adding ½ cup frozen peas for the last 2 minutes of cooking. Drain and return the pasta and peas to the pan. Add the finely grated rind of 1 lemon and 2 tablespoons lemon juice. Use a vegetable peeler to slice 2 zucchini into long ribbons. Add to the pan with 3 cups arugula, 2 tablespoons olive oil, and ¼ cup grated Parmesan cheese. Season to taste, divide among bowls, and top with a spoonful of ricotta cheese.

 Mushrooms Stuffed with Zucchini and Ricotta Brush a little olive oil over 4 large portobello mushrooms and place on a baking sheet, stem side up. Grate 1 zucchini and squeeze to remove any excess moisture, then mix with 1 cup ricotta cheese, 4 chopped sun-dried tomatoes, and ¼ cup chopped, pitted ripe black olives. Season and spoon onto the mushrooms, then sprinkle with ¼ cup grated Parmesan cheese. Place in a preheated oven, at 400°F, for 15 minutes, until golden and cooked through. Serve with ciabatta rolls.

30 Tortilla with Tomato and Arugula Salad

Serves 4

¼ cup olive oil
1 onion, finely chopped
3 potatoes, thickly sliced
1 cup water
5 eggs, beaten
4 cups arugula
2 tablespoons extra virgin olive oil
2 tablespoons lemon juice
6 cherry or plum tomatoes
handful of Parmesan cheese
    shavings
salt and black pepper

- Heat the olive oil in a large, nonstick skillet. Add the onion and potato and cook for 5–10 minutes, until golden, then pour in the measured water. Simmer gently until the potatoes are tender, then pour away any excess liquid.

- Season the eggs well, then pour into the skillet and stir gently. Cook over gentle heat for 10–15 minutes, until set all the way through, finishing off under a preheated broiler to set the top, if necessary.

- Toss the arugula with the extra virgin olive oil, lemon juice, and tomatoes. Season well and add the Parmesan shavings. Cut the tortilla into wedges and serve topped with the salad.

Egg, Tomato, and Arugula Wraps
Crack 4 eggs into a lightly greased, nonstick skillet. Dot with ¼ cup mascarpone cheese and season well. Cook over gentle heat for 2–3 minutes, until starting to set. Stir in 1 chopped tomato and cook for another 1 minute, until just set. Spoon the mixture over 4 wheat tortilla wraps, then sprinkle with 3 cups arugula and a little crumbled goat cheese. Wrap up the tortillas and serve.

Baked Eggs with Spicy Tomato and Arugula Sauce Mix 1¼ cups store-bought tomato sauce with 5 cups coarsely chopped arugula and a pinch of dried red pepper flakes. Spoon into 4 greased ramekins. Crack an egg into each ramekin, drizzle with a little olive oil, and sprinkle with some grated Parmesan cheese. Place in a preheated oven, at 400°F, for 15 minutes or until the eggs are just set.

ONE-VEGE-DER

Spicy Sweet Potato and Feta Salad

Serves 4

⅓ cup olive oil

2 sweet potatoes, thinly sliced

1 tablespoon white wine vinegar

1 (5 oz) package baby spinach leaves

1 tablespoon finely chopped red onion

1 cup crumbled feta cheese

1 red chile, sliced

½ cup pitted ripe black olives

salt and black pepper

- Toss 2 tablespoons of the oil with the sweet potatoes. Season well and cook in a preheated, hot ridged grill pan for 3 minutes on each side, until tender and lightly browned.

- Meanwhile, mix together the remaining oil with the white wine vinegar and season to taste. Toss with the spinach and red onion and arrange on serving plates. Arrange with the sweet potatoes, feta, chile, and olives and serve immediately.

 Baked Sweet Potatoes with Spicy Feta Filling Pierce 4 large sweet potatoes 2 or 3 times with a fork. Microwave on medium power for 5 minutes, until starting to soften. Rub all over with 2 teaspoons olive. Place in a preheated oven, at 425°F, for 10–15 minutes, until the skin is crisp and the potatoes cooked through. Cut a cross in each potato, open out, and divide ⅓ cup feta cheese, 3 cups arugula, 1 finely chopped red chile, and ¼ cup sliced ripe black olives between them. Drizzle with olive oil and serve immediately.

 Spicy Sweet Potato and Feta Casserole Place 1¾ lb peeled and sliced sweet potatoes in a shallow, flameproof casserole dish with 1¼ cups heavy cream and 1 seeded and finely chopped red chile. Season to taste and simmer for 15 minutes, until tender. Meanwhile, place 1 (6 oz) package fresh spinach in a strainer and pour boiling water over it until wilted, then squeeze thoroughly to remove excess water. Stir into the dish. Sprinkle with 1 cup dried white bread crumbs and ½ cup crumbled feta cheese. Drizzle with 2 tablespoons olive oil, then cook under a preheated hot broiler for 3 minutes, until golden.

QuickCook
Desserts

Recipes listed by cooking time

30

20

10

 # Crunchy Berry Brûlée

Serves 4

1 cup mascarpone cheese
1¼ cups store-bought vanilla
   pudding
1 cup mixed berries
½ cup granulated sugar
1½ tablespoons water

- Beat the mascarpone until smooth, then gently stir in the pudding and transfer the mixture to a serving dish. Sprinkle the berries on top.

- Place the sugar and measured water in a small, heavy saucepan and slowly bring to a boil, carefully swirling the pan from time to time. Keep cooking until the sugar dissolves and turns a deep caramel color. Pour the syrup over the berries and let rest for a few minutes to harden.

 ### Peach and Berry Cream Crunch

Peel, pit, and chop 2 peaches and arrange in a shallow, flameproof dish, then sprinkle with 1 cup mixed berries. Spoon 1¼ cups crème fraîche or Greek yogurt over them, then top with ½ cup raw sugar to completely cover the crème fraîche or yogurt. Place as close as you can to a preheated hot broiler and cook for 2–3 minutes, until the sugar has caramelized.

 ### Melting Berry Yogurt

Place 1¾ cups mixed berries in a serving dish. Spoon 1¼ cups plain yogurt over them, then sprinkle with ⅓ cup firmly packed dark brown sugar. Chill in the refrigerator for 20–25 minutes, until the sugar has melted.

 Apple and Orange Tart

Serves 4

1 sheet ready-to-bake puff
pastry
5 apples, such as Pippins, cored
and thinly sliced
6 tablespoons granulated sugar
finely grated rind of 1 orange

- Place the pastry on a baking sheet and use a sharp knife to lightly score a ½ inch border around the edges, being careful not to cut right through the pastry. Prick all over the center of the pastry with a fork.

- Toss the apples with 5 tablespoons of the sugar and the orange rind, then arrange on top of the pastry. Sprinkle the remaining sugar over the top. Place in a preheated oven, at 425°F, for 20 minutes, until the apples are tender and the pastry is crisp.

 Apple and Orange Compote

Heat 2 tablespoons butter in a skillet. Add 2 peeled, cored, and sliced Pippin apples and cook for 3 minutes, stirring frequently. Stir in 2 tablespoons granulated sugar and the finely grated rind and juice of 1 orange. Continue to cook for about 5 minutes, until the apples are tender and the sauce is syrupy. Mix ½ teaspoon ground cinnamon with ⅔ cup plain yogurt and serve with the compote.

 Apple and Orange Brioche Tarts

Cut out a circle from each of 4 slices of brioche, using a cup as a guide. Butter both sides and arrange on a baking sheet. Mix ¼ cup ground almonds (almond meal) and ¼ cup granulated sugar with 3 tablespoons mascarpone cheese and the finely grated rind of ½ orange, then spoon onto the brioche. Arrange 2 cored and thinly sliced apples on top, then sprinkle with 2 tablespoons granulated sugar. Place in a preheated oven, at 400°F, for 15–20 minutes, until golden.

 # Strawberry Cream Puffs

Serves 4

1 sheet ready-to-bake
  puff pastry
¼ cup confectioners' sugar
1¼ cups heavy cream
2 cups hulled and halved
  strawberries

- Cut the pastry into 12 equal rectangles and arrange on a baking sheet, then place another baking sheet on top. Place in a preheated oven, at 400°F, for 10 minutes, until golden and crisp.

- Sift half the confectioners' sugar over the pastry puffs and cook under a preheated hot broiler for 30 seconds, until the sugar melts. Let cool.

- Beat the cream with the remaining confectioners' sugar until soft peaks form. Arrange the pastry strips, whipped cream, and strawberries on plates and serve immediately.

 Strawberry Cream Desserts

Beat 1¼ cups heavy cream with ½ teaspoon vanilla extract and 2 tablespoons confectioners' sugar until soft peaks form. Stir in 1¼ cups hulled and chopped strawberries and divide among small glass bowls. Serve with shortbread cookies.

 Strawberry Cream Tart

Spread ¼ cup strawberry jam or preserves over the bottom of a store-bought pie crust. Beat 1¼ cups heavy cream with 3 tablespoons confectioners' sugar, 4 eggs, and 1 teaspoon vanilla extract and pour into the pie crust. Place in a preheated oven, at 350°F, for 25 minutes, until golden and just set. Sprinkle with hulled and chopped strawberries to serve.

ONE-PUDD-SUG

Syrup Sponge Dessert

Serves 6

1½ sticks butter, softened, plus
    extra for greasing
1 cup granulated sugar
1⅓ cups all-purpose flour
1 tablespoon baking powder
3 eggs
1 teaspoon vanilla extract
3 tablespoons milk
finely grated rind of ½ lemon
⅓ cup light corn syrup
cream, ice cream, or custard,
    to serve

- Grease a 1¼ quart deep, round ovenproof dish. Place all the ingredients, except the light corn syrup, in a food processor and blend until smooth. Spoon ¼ cup of the light corn syrup into the bottom of the dish, then add the batter and smooth the surface with a knife.

- Cover with microwave-proof plastic wrap and pierce the wrap a couple of times with a sharp knife. Cook in a microwave oven on medium heat for about 12 minutes. Test to see if itis cooked by inserting a toothpick or the tines of a fork into the dessert; it should come out clean.

- Let rest for 3 minutes, then turn out onto a deep plate and spoon over the remaining light corn syrup. Serve with cream, ice cream, or custard.

 Syrup-Topped Hotcakes

Place 1⅔ cups all-purpose flour in a food processor with 1 tablespoon baking powder, 2 eggs, 1 cup milk, and a pinch of salt and blend until smooth. Heat a large, nonstick skillet. Add a little butter and swirl around the skillet, then add generous tablespoonfuls of the batter. Cook for 2 minutes, until starting to set, then turn over and cook for another 1 minute. Remove from the skillet, keep warm, and repeat with the remaining batter. Serve the cakes sprinkled with blueberries and drizzled generously with light corn syrup.

 Syrup Sponge Desserts with

Ginger Make the sponge batter following the main recipe, adding 1 teaspoon ground ginger. Generously grease 6 dariole molds or ramekins with butter and place a small circle of wax paper in the bottom of each. Mix ¼ cup light corn syrup with 2 teaspoons chopped preserved ginger and a little of the syrup from the jar. Spoon into the molds and top with the batter. Place in a preheated oven, at 350°F, for 15–20 minutes, until cooked through and springy to the touch. Let rest in the molds for 3 minutes, then turn out onto serving plates and serve drizzled with more corn syrup.

10 Cinnamon-Spiced Cherries

Serves 4

2 tablespoons granulated sugar

1½ cups rosé wine

strip of pared lemon rind

1 cinnamon stick

3 cups cherries (about 1 lb),
  pitted if desired

- Combine all the ingredients in a saucepan. Bring to a boil, then reduce the heat and simmer for 5 minutes, until the sugar has dissolved and the cherries are tender.

- Use a slotted spoon to transfer the cherries to a serving dish, then cook the liquid over high heat for 3–4 minutes, until syrupy. Remove the cinnamon and lemon rind, then pour over the cherries and serve warm or cold.

 ## 20 Cherry and Cinnamon Soup

Heat 2 cups fruity white wine in a saucepan with ⅓ cup granulated sugar, 1 cinnamon stick, 1 strip of pared orange rind, and a good squeeze of juice. Simmer for 10 minutes, then add 3 cups pitted cherries (1 lb) and cook for 5 minutes, until tender. Remove the orange rind and cinnamon, add ⅔ cup mascarpone cheese, and puree with a handheld electric blender until smooth. Add a few ice cubes to cool the soup, then spoon into serving bowls and sprinkle with chocolate shavings and a few more pitted cherries.

 ## 30 Cherry and Cinnamon Cookies

Beat 2 sticks softened butter with ¾ cup granulated sugar. Stir in 1 egg yolk, then fold in 2⅓ cups all-purpose flour and 1 teaspoon ground cinnamon. Finally, add ⅓ cup dried cherries. Divide into 12 large balls and place on a baking sheet lined with wax paper, well spaced apart. Bake in a preheated oven, at 350°F, for 12–15 minutes, until just cooked. Let cool on a wire rack, then serve sandwiched together with scoops of vanilla ice cream.

30 Chocolate Fudge Brownie

Serves 8

1¾ sticks butter
8 oz semisweet chocolate, chopped
¾ cup firmly packed dark brown sugar
¾ cup granulated sugar
4 eggs, beaten
½ cup ground almonds (almond meal)
⅔ cup all-purpose flour
vanilla ice cream, to serve

- Gently melt the butter and chocolate in an ovenproof skillet, about 9 inches across. Remove from the heat and let cool for a couple of minutes.

- Beat together the sugars and eggs, then stir in the chocolate mixture followed by the almonds and flour.

- Wipe the rim of the skillet with a damp piece of paper towel to neaten, then pour the batter into the skillet. Place in a preheated oven, at 350°F, for 25 minutes, until just set. Serve warm with vanilla ice cream.

1 Malted Brownie Sundaes

Bring ⅔ cup heavy cream to a boil in a small, heavy saucepan. Remove from the heat and stir in 4 oz chopped semisweet chocolate until smooth. Cut 8 oz store-bought brownies into small squares and place in the bottom of sundae glasses. Add 2 scoops of vanilla ice cream to each glass, then drizzle with the chocolate sauce. Coarsely crush 24 malted milk balls and sprinkle them over the top to serve.

2 Brownie Lollipop Bites

Press 8 oz store-bought brownies into 20 small balls. Spear each one on a thin lollipop stick and place in the freezer for 10 minutes until firm. Bring ½ cup heavy cream to a boil in a small, heavy saucepan. Remove from the heat and stir in 2 oz chopped chocolate until smooth. Dip the lollipops in the melted chocolate, transfer to a baking sheet lined with wax paper, and let cool and harden.

ONE-PUDD-LAD

Tropical Fruit Salad

Serves 4

2 lemon grass stalks, coarsely
  chopped
⅔ cup water
¾ cup granulated sugar
1 cup peeled and sliced pineapple
1 mango, peeled and sliced
½ papaya, peeled and chopped
coconut macaroons, to serve

- Place the lemon grass, measured water, and sugar in a small, heavy saucepan, bring to a boil, and cook for 1 minute. Transfer to the freezer for about 10 minutes, until cool.

- Arrange the fruit in a serving bowl. Strain the syrup over the fruit and serve with macaroons or coconut ice cream.

Tropical Fruit with Lemon Sugar

Mix 2 tablespoons raw sugar with the finely grated rind of 1 lemon and a handful of chopped mint. Arrange a mixture of peeled and sliced tropical fruits on serving plates, then sprinkle with the sugar to serve.

Sticky Coconut Rice with Tropical

Fruit Cook 1 cup short-grain rice in a large saucepan of boiling water according to the package directions. Transfer to a colander to drain. Add ⅓ cup coconut milk, 3 tablespoons granulated sugar, and 1 lemon grass stalk to the pan and heat through. Return the rice to the pan, stir well, and set aside for 10 minutes to cool. Peel and cut 1 mango and ½ pineapple into thin slices and serve with the coconut rice, topped with a sprinkling of dried coconut.

1 Rum and Raisin French Toast

Serves 4

4 eggs, beaten
1 teaspoon vanilla extract
⅓ cup light cream
¼ cup rum
½ teaspoon ground cinnamon
4 thick slices of raisin bread, halved
2 tablespoons butter

- Mix together the eggs, vanilla extract, cream, rum, and cinnamon. Dip the raisin bread slices in the mixture and let soak for 2 minutes.

- Heat a large, nonstick skillet. Add a little butter and swirl around the skillet. Cook the bread for 2–3 minutes on each side, until golden.

Rum and Raisin Banana Sundaes

Soak 3 tablespoons raisins in ¼ cup rum. Place ½ cup granulated sugar in a small, heavy saucepan. Bring to a boil over low heat, then simmer until it starts to turn a dark caramel color. Remove from the heat. Carefully add ¼ cup heavy cream (it will spit), followed by the rum and raisin mixture. Return to the heat and stir until smooth. Halve 4 bananas lengthwise and arrange in serving bowls. Scoop some vanilla ice cream on top, then pour over the rum and raisin sauce.

Rum and Raisin Apple Charlotte

Peel, core, and chop 4 small apples and mix with ⅓ cup store-bought applesauce, 2 tablespoons rum, and 3 tablespoons raisins. Place in a shallow ovenproof dish, cover with aluminum foil, and cook in a preheated oven, at 400°F, for 15 minutes, until the apples are tender. Butter 6 slices of brioche and cut in half, then remove the foil and arrange over the apples. Sprinkle with ¼ cup raw sugar, then return to the oven for 10 minutes, until crisp.

30 Rhubarb and Ginger Slump

Serves 4–6

1½ lb rhubarb, trimmed and cut into chunks

1 tablespoon all-purpose flour

¼ cup granulated sugar

2 pieces of preserved ginger in syrup, drained and chopped, plus 2 tablespoons syrup from the jar

Topping

¾ cup all-purpose flour

1 teaspoon baking powder

6 tablespoons butter, softened

⅓ cup granulated sugar

¼ cup milk

1 egg, beaten

- Place the rhubarb, flour, sugar, and ginger in a shallow ovenproof dish and toss together. Cover with aluminum foil and place in a preheated oven, at 375°F, for 3 minutes.

- Meanwhile, place the ingredients for the topping in a food processor and blend until smooth. Uncover the rhubarb and spoon the topping over the fruit.

- Return to the oven for another 25 minutes or until the topping is golden and cooked through.

 Rhubarb and Ginger Desserts

Beat 1 cup heavy cream until soft peaks form, then stir in 1 tablespoon confectioners' sugar. Gently stir in ½ cup stewed, chopped sweetened rhubarb and divide among serving bowls. Crumble 1 ginger cookie over each portion and serve immediately.

 Rhubarb and Ginger Cream Baskets Stir 3 tablespoons melted butter with ¼ cup granulated sugar, 1½ tablespoons light corn syrup, ½ tablespoon heavy cream, and ⅓ cup all-purpose flour until smooth. Drop tablespoonfuls of the batter, well spaced apart, on a baking sheet lined with wax paper. Place in a preheated oven, at 350°F, for 5–10 minutes, until golden. Remove from the oven and drape the cookies over lightly oiled teacups while they are still hot. Let rest until crisp and set. Beat ⅔ cup heavy cream until soft peaks form, then stir in 1 chopped piece of preserved ginger and 1 tablespoon syrup from the jar. Spoon into the baskets, top each with a spoonful of stewed, sweetened rhubarb, and serve immediately.

Choc-Chip Ice Cream Sandwiches

**Serves 4
(with leftover cookies)**

1¼ sticks butter, softened

½ cup granulated sugar

½ cup firmly packed light brown sugar

1 egg, beaten

1⅓ cups all-purpose flour

1 teaspoon baking powder

1 teaspoon vanilla extract

½ cup mixed dark, milk, and white chocolate chips

4 scoops of vanilla ice cream

- Line a baking sheet with parchment paper. Beat the butter and sugars until light and fluffy, then stir in the egg. Beat in the flour, baking powder, and vanilla extract, then stir in three-quarters of the chocolate chips.

- Use a teaspoon to put 24 walnut-size balls of dough, well spaced apart, onto the baking sheet and flatten gently. Sprinkle with the remaining chocolate chips and cook in the preheated oven, at 375°F, for 8–10 minutes, until golden and just cooked through.

- Let the cookies cool on a wire rack, then serve 2 to each person, sandwiched together with a scoop of vanilla ice cream.

Quick Choc-Chip Ice Cream Sandwiches with Chocolate Sauce
Sandwich together 8 store-bought choc-chip cookies in pairs with 4 scoops of vanilla ice cream. Bring ⅔ cup heavy cream to a boil in a small, heavy saucepan, then pour it over 2 tablespoons granulated sugar and 4 oz chopped semisweet chocolate in a heatproof bowl. Stir until smooth, then drizzle it over the sandwiches to serve.

Choc-Chip Scone Sandwiches
Mix 3⅔ cups all-purpose flour in a mixing bowl with 1 tablespoon granulated sugar, 1½ tablespoons baking powder, 1 teaspoon baking soda, and a pinch of salt. Rub in 1 stick diced cold butter with fingertips until the mixture resembles fine bread crumbs. Stir in 1¼ cups buttermilk and ½ cup chocolate chips. Bring the dough together, then turn out onto a lightly floured surface and press down until uniformly about 1¼ inches thick. Cut out scones with a 2 inch round cutter, piling up and pressing down the scraps to cut out more scones. Place on a lightly floured baking sheet, brush with beaten egg yolk, and cook in a preheated oven, at 425°F, for 12–15 minutes, until cooked through. Let cool. Beat 1¼ cups heavy cream until soft peaks form, then stir in 1 teaspoon vanilla extract and confectioners' sugar to taste. Split the scones and fill with the cream to serve.

Baked Figs with Honey and Pistachios

Serves 4

12 figs
2 tablespoons butter, plus extra
    for greasing
2 tablespoons firmly packed
    light brown sugar
2 tablespoons honey
3 tablespoons orange juice
½ teaspoon ground cinnamon
¼ cup shelled, unsalted
    pistachio nuts
plain yogurt, to serve

- Lightly grease a small, shallow roasting pan. Cut a cross down into the top of each fig, then arrange them in the pan. Place a little butter on each, then pour the sugar, honey, orange juice, and cinnamon over the fruit.

- Place in a preheated oven, at 400°F, for 12 minutes, then sprinkle with the pistachios and return to the oven for another 3 minutes, until the figs are tender. Serve with plain yogurt.

Broiled Figs with Honey Mascarpone and Pistachio Biscotti Cut 12 figs in half and arrange, cut sides up, on a broiler pan. Place a pat of butter on top of each and sprinkle with ½ teaspoon ground cinnamon. Cook under a preheated hot broiler for 5 minutes, until tender. Mix ⅔ cup mascarpone cheese with 1 tablespoon honey and ½ teaspoon vanilla extract. Serve the hot figs with the mascarpone and some pistachio biscotti.

Fig, Honey, and Pistachio Tarts Cut out 4 circles about 5 inches across from 1 sheet ready-to-bake puff pastry. Arrange on a lightly greased baking sheet and crimp the edges. Process ¾ cup shelled, unsalted pistachio nuts in a food processor until smooth, then mix with 1 egg yolk, 1 tablespoon firmly packed light brown sugar, and 1 tablespoon honey. Spread the mixture over the centers of the pastries, then arrange 2 sliced figs on top of each. Place in a preheated oven, at 425°F, for 20 minutes, until golden and cooked through. Drizzle with a little more honey to serve.

Chocolate Fondue with Marshmallows

Serves 4

1¼ cups heavy cream

2 tablespoons orange liqueur (optional)

5 oz semisweet chocolate, chopped

5 oz milk chocolate, chopped

marshmallows, cookies, and miniature doughnuts, to serve

- Bring the cream to a boil in a small, heavy saucepan. Remove from the heat and stir in the liqueur, if using, and the chocolate until melted. Transfer to a warm serving bowl or fondue pot, if desired.

- Arrange the marshmallows, cookies, and miniature doughnuts on a serving plate, spear them on long forks, and dip them into the warm chocolate.

Chocolate and Marshmallow

Trifle Place 3 cups miniature marshmallows, 4 tablespoons butter, and 8 oz chopped chocolate in a heavy saucepan and melt over low heat until smooth. Stand the pan in a bowl of cold water and let cool for 5–10 minutes. Beat 1 cup heavy cream until it holds its shape, then stir in 1 teaspoon vanilla extract and the cooled chocolate mixture. Arrange bite-size chunks of plain cake in the bottom of a serving dish and spoon the chocolate mixture on top. Sprinkle with a handful of raspberries and blueberries to serve.

Chocolate Cupcakes with Melting Marshmallows

Place ⅔ cup light brown sugar, ¾ cup all-purpose flour, ½ cup unsweetened cocoa powder, and 2 teaspoons baking powder in a large bowl. Stir in 3 eggs, ½ cup vegetable oil, 2 tablespoons milk, and ¼ cup chocolate chips. Spoon the batter into a 12 cup muffin pan with cupcake liners. Place in a preheated oven, at 350°F, for 20 minutes. Top the cupcakes with ½ cup miniature marshmallows and place under a preheated hot broiler for 1 minute until lightly browned.

Boozy Caramelized Oranges

Serves 4

4 oranges
1 cup granulated sugar
¼ cup water
3 tablespoons orange liqueur

- Peel the oranges and cut into thick slices, reserving any juice. Place the sugar in a heavy saucepan with the measured water. Cook over medium heat until it starts to turn a dark brown color.

- Remove from the heat and carefully pour in the liqueur (it will spit). The caramel will harden, so return to a low heat and cook until melted again. Stir in the oranges and any juice, then spoon into glass bowls and serve.

Boozy Caramel and Orange Trifle

Heat 1 cup sugar and ⅓ cup water in a heavy saucepan until golden brown. Remove from the heat, add 2 tablespoons butter and 1 cup heavy cream, and set aside to cool. Beat 1 cup heavy cream with 3 tablespoons confectioners' sugar until soft peaks form. Arrange 12–14 ladyfingers in the bottom of a serving bowl, then pour ¼ cup orange juice and 1 tablespoon orange liqueur of them. Spoon the cream on top. Arrange 2 oranges, peeled and cut into segments, over the cream, then drizzle with the caramel sauce. Serve sprinkled with toasted almonds.

Crêpes Suzette

Place 1¼ cups all-purpose flour, 1 cup milk, 1 egg, and a pinch of sugar in a food processor and blend until smooth. Heat a nonstick skillet and add a little butter. Swirl around the skillet, then add a ladleful of batter. Cook for 1 minute, until set, then turn over and cook for another 30 seconds. Fold into quarters, set aside, and repeat with the remaining batter. Add ¼ cup granulated sugar and 3 tablespoons water to the skillet and cook until the sugar turns golden. Remove from the heat and add ⅔ cup fresh orange juice and 2 tablespoons orange liqueur. Return to a low heat and cook until smooth, then add the folded crepes and heat through, spooning over the sauce.

ONE-PUDD-MOK

30 Tiramisu

Serves 4

1 cup heavy cream
¼ cup Marsala
1 cup mascarpone cheese
¼ cup confectioners' sugar
1 teaspoon vanilla extract
1¼ cups very strong coffee,
 cooled
20 ladyfingers
3 tablespoons grated semisweet
 chocolate, to decorate

- Beat the cream until stiff peaks form. Reserve 1 tablespoon of the Marsala, then stir the remaining Marsala into the cream with the mascarpone, 3 tablespoons of the confectioners' sugar, and the vanilla extract.

- Stir the remaining Marsala and confectioners' sugar into the coffee, then dip 4 of the ladyfingers into the mixture and place each in the bottom of a glass or small serving dish. They should be just soft, not soggy.

- Spoon some of the creamy mixture on top, then repeat the layers to use up the remaining ingredients. Chill in the refrigerator for 20 minutes, then serve sprinkled with grated chocolate.

1 Creamy Coffee Martinis

Beat ½ cup heavy cream with 2 tablespoons Marsala until slightly thickened. Stir together 1 cup cooled coffee with ⅓ cup coffee liqueur and 1 tablespoon confectioners' sugar. Pour into 4 cocktail glasses, top with the thickened cream, then grate a little chocolate over the top and serve with ladyfingers.

2 Tiramisu Cupcakes

Place 1 stick butter, ½ cup firmly packed light brown sugar, ¾ cup all-purpose flour, and 1 teaspoon baking powder in a food processor with 1 egg, 1 egg yolk, and ⅓ cup cooled strong coffee and blend until smooth. Spoon the batter into a 12-cup muffin pan lined with paper liners and place in a preheated oven, at 350°F, for 15–18 minutes, until a toothpick inserted into the cakes comes out clean.

3⓵ Prune Clafoutis

Serves 4

butter, for greasing
3 eggs
⅔ cup granulated sugar
⅓ cup all-purpose flour
⅔ cup heavy cream
⅔ cup milk
1 teaspoon vanilla extract
½ cup pitted prunes

- Lightly grease a shallow ovenproof dish. Beat together the eggs and sugar until pale, frothy, and tripled in volume. Sift the flour into the bowl and lightly fold in. Add the cream, milk, and vanilla extract and mix until just combined.

- Pour into the ovenproof dish and place in a preheated oven, at 375°F, for 5 minutes, until the surface is just starting to set. Sprinkle with the prunes, then return to the oven for another 15–20 minutes, until the clafoutis is risen and golden.

1⓵ Creamy Plum and Port Desserts

Beat 1¼ cups heavy cream until soft peaks form, then stir in ¼ cup port, 6 pitted and chopped plums, and a little granulated sugar to taste. Divide the creamy mixture among serving glasses.

2⓵ Plum Crisp

Halve and pit 4 plums and place in a lightly greased ovenproof dish. Cut 2 tablespoons butter into small pieces and sprinkle them over the plums with 2 tablespoons granulated sugar. Cover with aluminum foil and place in a preheated oven, at 400°F, for 10 minutes. Meanwhile, crush 18 gingersnaps (1 cup crushed) and mix with 2 tablespoons softened butter. Remove the foil and sprinkle the cookie mixture over the plums. Return to the oven for another 5 minutes, until lightly crisp.

ONE-PUDD-WAO

Passionfruit and Mango with Meringue

Serves 4

1¼ cups heavy cream

2–3 tablespoons confectioners' sugar

4 meringue nests, crushed

1 mango, peeled and sliced

1 passionfruit, halved

- Beat the cream with the confectioners' sugar until it just holds its shape. Gently stir in the meringue, most of the mango, and a little of the passionfruit pulp. Spoon into glasses and top with the remaining fruit.

2 Passionfruit and Mango Cream

Peel and chop 1 mango and divide among 4 glasses. Beat 1 egg yolk with 2 tablespoons granulated sugar until frothy and pale, then stir in the pulp of 2 passionfruit. Beat 1 cup heavy cream until soft peaks form, then stir into the egg mixture and beat until thickened. Add 1 tablespoon orange liqueur and 4 crushed meringue nests. Spoon the mixture over the mango and top with a little more chopped fruit, if desired.

3 Passionfruit Meringue Desserts

Bring ⅔ cup light cream and 1 cup milk to a boil in a heavy saucepan. Meanwhile, beat 4 egg yolks with ⅓ cup granulated sugar. Carefully stir in the hot milk, then add 2 cups fresh white bread crumbs and the pulp of 4 passionfruit. Divide among four 1 cup ramekins and place in a preheated oven, at 325°F, for 20 minutes, until just set. Meanwhile, beat the 4 egg whites until stiff, then slowly beat in ¼ cup superfine or granulated sugar until glossy and smooth. Spoon the mixture over the desserts and return to the oven for 3–5 minutes, until lightly golden.

30 Peach and Raspberry Melba

Serves 4

1 cup water
²/₃ cup granulated sugar
1 vanilla bean
4 peaches, halved and pitted
8 scoops of vanilla ice cream
1 cup raspberries
cookie curls, to serve

- Place the measured water, sugar, and vanilla extract in a saucepan, cook over low heat until the sugar dissolves, then cook over high heat for 5–10 minutes, until syrupy.

- Add the peach halves and cook for another 5 minutes, until tender, then let cool. Remove the skins and thinly slice the peaches.

- Arrange the peach slices, ice cream, and half the raspberries in sundae glasses. Press the remaining raspberries through a strainer to make a coulis, drizzle it over the top of the sundaes, and serve with cookie curls.

Caramelized Peaches with Mascarpone and Raspberries
Tightly fit 4 halved and pitted peaches into an ovenproof dish, cut sides up. Sprinkle with 2 tablespoons sugar, then place 1 tablespoon mascarpone cheese into the hollow of each peach half. Sprinkle with ¾ cup raspberries, followed by another 2 tablespoons sugar. Cook under a preheated hot broiler for 3–5 minutes, until golden and bubbling.

Baked Peaches and Raspberries
Place 4 halved and pitted peaches in an ovenproof dish. Pour over ¹/₃ cup orange juice, and add 2 tablespoons orange liqueur, if desired. Dot a little butter on each peach, then sprinkle with 2 tablespoons granulated sugar. Place in a preheated oven, at 400°F, for 15 minutes, then sprinkle with 1 cup raspberries and return to the oven for another 3 minutes, until tender and lightly caramelized. Serve with vanilla ice cream.

ONE-PUDD-HYZ

# Apricot and Almond Crostata

Serves 6–8

butter, for greasing
confectioners' sugar, for dusting
1 sheet store-bought rolled dough
   pie crust
5 oz marzipan, sliced
8 apricots, halved and pitted
¼ cup slivered almond
2 tablespoons milk
2 tablespoons granulated sugar
cream or ice cream, to serve

- Lightly grease a baking sheet. Dust a work surface with confectioners' sugar, then roll out the dough into a 14 inch circle. Place on the baking sheet, arrange the marzipan slices in the middle, and top with the halved apricots.

- Sprinkle the almonds over the top, then fold the edges of the pastry up and over to form a rough border. Brush the pastry border with the milk and sprinkle with the granulated sugar. Place in a preheated oven, at 400°F, for 25 minutes, until the pastry is just cooked through. Serve with cream or ice cream.

1 Apricot and Almond Desserts

Place 4 apricots in a small saucepan with ½ cup apple juice and heat until softened. Break 4 almond biscotti into small pieces and place in serving glasses. Spoon the warm apricots over them along with a little almond liqueur, if desired. Top each with 2 tablespoons Greek yogurt and a handful of toasted slivered almond.

2 Baked Apricots Stuffed with

Almonds Place 25 amaretti cookies (about 4 oz) in a food processor with ¼ cup blanched almonds, 1 egg white, and 2 tablespoons sugar and pulse to form a rough paste. Halve 9 apricots, and arrange, cut sides up, in a shallow ovenproof dish, then place a little of the almond mixture on top of each apricot. Place in a preheated oven, at 400°F, for 10–15 minutes, until the fruit is tender and the topping is crisp.

 # Creamy Chocolate Pudding

Serves 4

⅓ cup granulated sugar

3 tablespoons cornstarch

¼ cup unsweetened
  cocoa powder

3 eggs

2 cups milk

3 oz milk chocolate, chopped

To serve

whipped cream

grated chocolate

- Place the sugar, cornstarch, and cocoa powder in a heatproof bowl and beat in the eggs. Bring the milk to a boil in a saucepan, then beat a little of it into the egg mixture. Transfer the chocolate mixture to the saucepan, stir well, and cook for 3–5 minutes, stirring continuously, until thickened.

- Place the chopped chocolate in the bowl, strain the chocolate pudding on top, and stir until smooth. Cover the surface with plastic wrap to prevent a skin from forming, then place in the freezer for 15 minutes, stirring occasionally, until cool.

- When the chocolate pudding is cool, divide among glass bowls, top with whipped cream, and sprinkle with grated chocolate.

 ### Creamy Chocolate Sauce with Brioche

Dunkers Bring ⅔ cup heavy cream to a boil in a small, heavy saucepan. Remove from the heat, add 4 oz chopped semisweet chocolate and stir until smooth. Halve 4 brioche rolls and lightly toast. Butter well and sprinkle with ½ teaspoon ground cinnamon. Dunk the brioche in the chocolate sauce to serve.

 ### Creamy Chocolate Truffles

Bring ⅓ cup heavy cream to a boil in a small, heavy saucepan. Place 5 oz chopped semisweet chocolate in a heatproof bowl with 2 tablespoons butter. Pour the cream over the chocolate and stir until smooth. Place in the freezer for 15 minutes, stirring occasionally, until the mixture has set. Use a teaspoon to scoop out pieces of the mixture, form into balls, and roll in unsweetened cocoa powder to serve.

Banana and Caramel Puffs

Serves 4

⅔ cup firmly packed light brown sugar

¼ cup water

2 tablespoons butter

1 sheet ready-to-bake puff pastry

2 bananas, sliced

- Heat the sugar and measured water in a large ovenproof skillet until golden and caramel colored. Carefully add the butter and swirl around the skillet until melted.

- Meanwhile, cut out 4 circles from the pastry using a 3 inch cookie cutter.

- Carefully arrange the banana slices in 4 circles in the caramel, then place a pastry circle on top of each. Place in a preheated oven, at 425°F, for 15 minutes, until puffed and cooked through. Use a spatula to turn out of the pan and drizzle with the remaining sauce.

Banana and Caramel Desserts

Slice 2 bananas and divide among glass serving bowls. Beat ⅔ cup heavy cream until soft peaks form, then stir in 1 tablespoon dulce de leche or other caramel sauce. Spoon the sauce over the banana, then drizzle with more dulce de leche and top with chopped pecan nuts.

Banana and Caramel Tart

Lay 1 sheet ready-to-bake puff pastry on a work surface, place an ovenproof skillet on top, and cut around it, leaving a ¾ inch border. Chill in the refrigerator until ready to use. Heat ⅔ cup firmly packed light brown sugar in the skillet with ½ cup water until the sugar melts and starts to turn golden. Remove from the heat. Halve 3 or 4 bananas lengthwise and arrange in the skillet until the bottom is almost covered. Lay the pastry on top and tuck in the edges. Place in a preheated oven, at 425°F, for 20 minutes or until golden and puffed.

30 Apple and Blackberry Strudels

Serves 4

6 tablespoons butter, melted
3 Granny Smith apples, peeled, cored, and thinly sliced
1 cup blackberries
½ cup granulated sugar
pinch of ground cinnamon
4 large sheets of phyllo pastry
confectioners' sugar, for dusting
heavy cream, whipped, to serve

- Mix together the apples, blackberries, sugar, and cinnamon. Unwrap the phyllo pastry and cover with damp paper towels until ready to use it.

- Working quickly, brush 1 sheet of pastry with the butter and arrange one-quarter of the apple mixture in a log shape along one short side, leaving a 1 inch space at each end. Fold the 2 long sides in over the mixture, then roll up the pastry to enclose it completely. Repeat with the remaining ingredients to make 4 rolls in all.

- Place the strudels on the baking sheet and cook in a preheated oven, at 400°F, for 15–20 minutes, until crisp. Serve with whipped heavy cream.

 Apple and Blackberry Desserts Beat 1¼ cups heavy cream until soft peaks form. Stir in ½ cup good-quality, store-bought applesauce. Spoon into serving dishes, top with a few blackberries, and dust with confectioners' sugar.

 Crunchy Apple and Blackberry Crisp Peel, core, and chop 4 Pippin apples. Place in an ovenproof dish and stir in the finely grated rind of 1 lemon, ¼ cup granulated sugar, 1 teaspoon vanilla extract, and ¼ cup water. Cover with aluminum foil and place in a preheated oven, at 375°F, for 15 minutes. Remove the foil, add 1 cup blackberries, and return to the oven for another 1 minute. Meanwhile, lightly crush 4 oz crumbly butter cookies, sprinkle with the fruit, and return to the oven for 1–2 minutes, until crisp.

ONE-PUDD-SAE

1 Lemon Syllabub

Serves 4

1¼ cups heavy cream
⅓ cup sweet white wine
¼ cup granulated sugar
finely grated rind and juice of
  ½ lemon

- Beat the cream until it just starts to hold its shape. Add the wine, one-third at a time, beating well between each addition.

- Stir in the sugar and lemon juice and continue beating until fluffy and thick. Spoon into glasses, sprinkle with lemon rind, and serve.

 Lemon Cheesecakes with Blueberries Place 1 cup blueberries in a small saucepan with 3 tablespoons granulated sugar and 2 tablespoons water and cook until the berries start to burst. Let cool. Meanwhile, mix 1 cup mascarpone cheese with 3 tablespoons confectioners' sugar and 2 tablespoons lemon juice. Crush 4 plain cookies and divide among glasses, then spoon the lemon mixture on top. Pour the cooled blueberries and their juice over the top and serve.

 Little Lemon Desserts Beat 4 tablespoons butter and ⅓ cup granulated sugar with the finely grated rind of 1 lemon until light and fluffy. Add 2 egg yolks and ¼ cup lemon juice. Stir in 1 tablespoon flour, then ½ cup heavy cream and ⅔ cup milk until smooth. Pour into 4 lightly greased 1 cup ramekins. Place the ramekins in a shallow roasting pan and pour boiling water into the pan until it comes halfway up the ramekins. Place in a preheated oven, at 350°F, for 20–25 minutes, until golden and slightly risen.

30 Crunchy Pear Crisp

Serves 6

6 pears, peeled, cored, and
  chopped
2 tablespoons firmly packed
  light brown sugar
½ teaspoon ground cinnamon
¼ cup water
cream, ice cream, or custard,
  to serve

Topping

⅓ cup firmly packed light brown
  sugar
½ teaspoon ground cinnamon
1⅓ cups rolled oats
⅔ cup all-purpose flour
6 tablespoons butter
1 tablespoon light corn syrup

- Place the pears in a shallow ovenproof dish with the sugar, cinnamon, and measured water and stir together. Cover with aluminum foil and place in a preheated oven, at 375°F, for 5 minutes.

- Meanwhile, make the crumb topping. Place the sugar in a food processor with the cinnamon, oats, flour, and butter and pulse until the mixture resembles fine bread crumbs. Alternatively, rub the butter into the dry ingredients with your fingertips. Stir the light corn syrup into the topping mixture.

- Remove the pears from the oven, uncover, and sprinkle the topping over them. Return to the oven for another 20–25 minutes or until bubbling and lightly browned. Serve warm with cream, ice cream, or custard.

10 Sautéed Pears with Crunchy Topping

Heat 2 tablespoons butter in a skillet. Add 6 pears, peeled, quartered, and cored, and cook for 5 minutes, turning often, until golden all over. Stir in ½ teaspoon ground cinnamon and ⅓ cup orange juice and cook until the liquid bubbles away. Divide among serving dishes, then sprinkle with 6 crushed oatmeal cookies mixed with ¼ cup chopped pecan nuts. Spoon over plain yogurt or whipped cream to serve.

20 Pear Crisp Tarts

Cut out six 4 inch circles from 2–3 sheets of ready-to-bake puff pastry, arrange on a lightly greased baking sheet, and place a thinly sliced pear on each one. Place ⅔ cup all-purpose flour in a mixing bowl with ⅓ cup sugar, ¼ cup slivered almonds, and ½ teaspoon ground cinnamon. Rub in 6 tablespoons diced butter with fingertips and sprinkle with the pears. Cook in a preheated oven, at 425°F, for 15 minutes, until puffed and golden.

ONE-PUDD-COW

Vanilla Zabaglione

Serves 4

6 egg yolks
¼ cup granulated sugar
1 vanilla bean
¼ cup Marsala or
   dessert wine
biscotti, to serve

- Place the egg yolks and sugar in a heatproof bowl. Split the vanilla bean lengthwise, scrape out the seeds, add to the bowl, and beat together. Place the bowl over a saucepan of gently simmering water, being careful that the bottom of the bowl does not touch the water.

- Add the Marsala and beat continuously with a handheld electric mixer for 5–8 minutes, until the mixture is frothy and thickened. It should leave a trail when you remove the beaters. Pour into glass serving bowls and serve with biscotti.

Vanilla Egg Nog

Bring 2 cups milk and 1 cup light cream to a boil in a heavy saucepan with 1 split vanilla bean. Beat 4 egg yolks with ⅓ cup granulated sugar in a heatproof bowl to combine, then pour on the hot milk and stir well. Return to the pan and cook over low heat for 5–10 minutes, until thickened. Place 4 oz chopped white chocolate in the mixing bowl with 2 tablespoons brandy, if desired. Pour over the thickened milk and stir until combined. Spoon into cups to serve.

Vanilla Zabaglione Cream

Make the Vanilla Zabaglione, as above, then chill in the refrigerator for 15 minutes. Beat 1 cup heavy cream until soft peaks form, then carefully stir in the cooled zabaglione. Transfer to a serving dish, sprinkle with fresh raspberries, and serve with tuille cookies.

ONE-PUDD-MEJ

Index

Page references in *italics* indicate photographs

Acknowledgments

Recipes by **Emma Lewis**
Executive Editor **Eleanor Maxfield**
Editor **Alex Stetter**
Copy Editor **Jo Smith**
Art Direction **Tracy Killick for Tracy Killick Art Direction and Design**
Original Design Concept **www.gradedesign.com**
Designers **Tracy Killick and Janis Utton for Tracy Killick Art Direction and Design**
Photographer **William Shaw**
Home Economists **Emma Jane Frost, Emma Lewis**
Stylist **Liz Hippisley**
Senior Production Controller **Caroline Alberti**